Jesus on the Way to Jerusalem

Letters from an Understanding Friend

Isaias Powers

TWENTY-THIRD PUBLICATIONS
Mystic, Connecticut

Third printing August 1985

Second Printing   February 1985

ISBN 0-89622-215-2
Library of Congress Catalog Card Number 84-50409

Edited and designed by John G. van Bemmel

Cover design by George Herrick

CONTENTS

INTRODUCTION

We have a high priest
who has passed into the heavens:
Jesus, the Son of God...
providing us with mercy and grace
in times of need.
For we do not have a high priest
who cannot have compassion on our
infirmities;
but one tried as we are
in all things, except sin...
Because he himself has suffered and been tempted,
he is able to help those who are tempted.

Hebrews 4:13-15, 2:18

Everyone likes to receive a good letter from a kind, understanding friend. It is especially appreciated when the friend seems to know what we are going through, when the letter speaks to the heart about problems of the heart.

The forty letters of this book have been written to provide such comfort. They are presented as though they have been written by our friend, who is also our Lord and Master and is now our high priest pleading for us before God, his Father.

He has known the sufferings we endure as we continue on our journey of life; he has known them all. Long before he met the ultimate test of love on Calvary, he experienced the more "ordinary" kinds of hurts, which tempted him to wonder, "Why should I continue?"

These more ordinary temptations are the considerations of this book. The plan is a simple one. Jesus is pictured as sitting down by himself, usually in the evening, writing about some incident that has just happened to him. He knows we will suffer under similiar circumstances. He assumes that "by the time the letter reaches us," we have already suffered. So he writes about how he is managing under

1

the stress of it, and how he wants us to manage under our stress.

The Gospel of St. Luke is the source for these letters. Tradition has it that Luke was a physician. Perhaps he was. If there were psychiatrists in his day, he would have been one. He was interested in the psychological implications of the events in our Lord's life. Luke is the only evangelist who adds this ominous note at the end of Christ's temptation in the desert (4: 1-13): "Then the devil left him for a more favorable opportunity." This phrase tells us there is no doubt that Jesus had not seen an end of his adversary. The tempter would continue until one of them was completely vanquished.

Satan's "further opportunities" are most strongly suggested in the last journey Jesus took. St. Luke repeats at least seven times the significant fact that certain painful events happened "as he was on his way to Jerusalem"; Jesus knew he would be put to death and be raised up on the third day:

Luke 9:52	(see Letter 1)
9:57	(see Letter 3)
10:30	(see Letter 6)
13:22	(see Letter 18)
17:11	(see Letter 27)
18:30	(third passion prediction)
19:11	(see Letter 31)

Because Luke was so insistent—and solemn—about his theme, we must realize that "more is going on" than what would first appear. As Jesus confronted his enemies, met ten lepers, or ate supper with Martha and Mary, he was not just experiencing some isolated incidents that could be forgotten in a day; he was feeling every adventure in the light of what he knew would be waiting for him at the end of his journey.

Jesus felt pain each time he was treated with hostility or disrespect. Yet he continued to love. He never gave in to discouragement.

See the Appendix for some reasons why Jesus had to feel pain in many ways, instead of avoiding discomforts or fighting back. You are asked to read the Appendix before you read the letters. It will be helpful. The book itself consists of letters presenting Jesus writing down his own thoughts, but the Appendix is a commentary about Jesus, why his love could not co-exist with the use of force. There was no place for such comments until our Lord finished what he had to say.

Sometimes it is easier for us to appreciate Christ's mercy and courage when we visualize him in settings we are more familiar with: a fireside chat, a visit home, a discussion about the latest news, a celebration with friends of some achievement.

It doesn't matter that there was no postal service two thousand years ago; that the English language was not invented yet; that words like "bingo," "commuting to work," "congressional inquest" are things appropriate to America, not to Judea or Galilee. An honest imagination can hurdle these technicalities.

Faith is the important thing. Faith tells us that we do have a high priest who is able to help us in times of our need. He is not one who cannot have compassion. He has known firsthand the hurts we have. Luke won't let us forget it.

It is good to get forty letters from such a kind, understanding friend. It is suggested that you read them one at a time. Read each one as you would read a letter in your mail box. Then reread those that seem especially meant for you, as situations come up.

Faith will inspire your love for Jesus, as you remember what he went through for love of you. Faith will help you understand that our Lord wants you to link your passion with his own. These personal letters will urge you to continue your work of love despite discouragements, despite your sufferings.

You have every reason to be confident. Jesus has called you, in forty different ways, to be his disciples. . .and his friends.

LETTER 1

When the days drew near for him to be lifted up, Jesus set his face to go to Jerusalem. And he sent messengers ahead of him, who went and entered a village of the Samaritans, to make ready for him; but the people would not receive him, because his face was set toward Jerusalem.

Luke 9:51-52

*　　　*　　　*

West of Capharnaum
Border of Samaria
Just before supper
April 28

Dear Disciple, my Friend,

Today is the beginning of my last journey. I'll end up in Jerusalem. There I'll be crucified; there, after my resurrection, I'll have my last words with my disciples before I return to my Father in heaven. Jerusalem's my destiny; there's no turning back. I'm determined to start the process of my final act of love.

I've decided something else, as well. Every now and then, I'll sit down and write you a letter. Not every day, but whenever the Spirit moves me to do so, and whenever I have the time.

Many reasons went into this decision. For one thing, writing helps me pray better. It also focuses my thoughts. It establishes constancy even more firmly in my heart, and gives meaning to my sufferings. As I put my thoughts on paper, I bend ideals back down to earth. By words, the Word of me is once again "made flesh."

You're my "flesh." You and all my disciples to be born are the reason I make this journey of love. Because I'm writing you these letters, I can "see" you better. I can know you are there...out there in the future.

5

I hope these letters will help you; I'm writing with you in mind. You'll know that I feel the same things you feel; I hurt from the same conditions that hurt you. You'll come to understand that I'm not only your Lord and friend. I'm also a "familiar" in your suffering. I'm not some imperturbable deity who can't have compassion on your distress. I've been there. I know the insides of loneliness and let-downs.

There's one more reason I decided to start writing letters. I have a little more time on my hands. Before today, my apostles were always crowding around me, telling me about the experiences of their last adventure, asking me questions about what I had said...things like that. But now I'm left alone much more than I used to be.

The atmosphere's rather glum. Andrew and Phillip are getting supper ready, meager as it is. My apostles are clustered around in their own group on the other side of the fire, arguing among themselves.

They're naturally upset. Short on supplies, they'd gone to buy some from a nearby Samaritan town, but were refused.

On previous occasions, they'd be all around me, asking me what to do, where to go next, whether we ought to retaliate. But they're not around me this evening. They're a little afraid of me now. They've been in shock since I told them I must set my face toward Jerusalem to be lifted up.

They understand my statement only in its dreadful aspect: lifted up on the cross. It'll be a long time before they understand that I also mean lifted up from death and then raised up to be with my Father in heaven. It'll be a long time before they understand.

They stay with me, but they do so reluctantly now. Gone is the joy they had in my presence, gone the thrill they experienced when they preached in my name. They're restive, anxious, cautious. I can sense it.

In a kind of quiet, undramatic way, the whole world is filling me with sadness. Nothing exactly that I can get a handle on...nothing that gives me cause to scream out in pain or challenge somebody. Just a heaviness in my heart; from all sides comes the dull repetition of nonacceptance.

The well-known among my people, of course, don't accept me. I realized that months ago. They envy me. They bitterly resent the words I speak and the good I do.

Now my apostles, my hand-picked friends, have changed. Their unhappy faces tell the story of their sadness...and my sorrow. They continue with me only because they hope I will change; they hope things will be like they were before.

Then, to top it all off, the Samaritans refuse me hospitality. They've already forgotten the good I've done for their people. Their bigotry has lumped me into their hatred of all Jews. So I'm stranded.

I used to think that even if my own people disowned me, others would appreciate what I am doing. Of course, some will...but I see it now: This one village is but a small clue of a large, prolonged, almost world-wide, snub. As long as the ages last, I'll be made to feel as unwelcome as I've been by this Samaritan town that has just refused to sell us groceries.

You know how it is. You've suffered from the same sadness; it sometimes thuds all around you. Certain people are your enemies. They have been, and probably always will be. You can handle that. But your friends—those you counted on—they sometimes treat you as though you had leprosy or something. All of a sudden, you're left alone, outside their care. They want you to change, to be different from what you know you must be. They can't understand you, and don't know how to understand you. You see them (or sense them) forming in their little groups and talking about you behind your back. This hurts. I know.

Then, to top it all off, people you meet for the first time rebuff you, also. It seems there's no place to turn. Nothing dramatic about it. At times, there's simply nowhere to go to find a way out of your loneliness.

Never mind. Join me when you feel what I'm feeling tonight. I experience this sorrow because I must. I must go to Jerusalem to prove my love.

Rejection by strangers and nonacceptance by friends is their response to me. I can't change them; I can't force anyone to love me or appreciate my purpose in life. If they refuse to understand, I'll simply have to suffer their refusal.

I'm asking you to do the same. You can't back out of love or back down from your ideals. If friends react discourteously, start giving you the cold shoulder or something, this can't be helped. If strangers don't give you a chance, if they lump you into their class hatred, or somehow distrust you before they even try to know you—never mind. You can't force people to change their opinions any more than I can.

I know what you're going through. I'm with you so that you don't become too saddened by it. When I've finished my course, I'll be with my Father. There I'll pray for you. My strength will be my gift to you...so that no put-downs by other people will cause you to give up on your work of love.

This will be my prayer for when you're lonely:

Lord God, my Father...look with love upon my disciples, my friends.

Life is not going well for them, right now. In addition to their enemies, the friends they counted on seem to be drifting out of their lives. And new friends, new ways of acceptance, are not available. They don't know where to turn. They have no choice but to suffer, to go through it.

Send me to them. Let them experience, as fully as they can, my good resolve to do your will...as I began my journey to Jerusalem.

Let them understand (more clearly now, *because* they suffer) that I am with them on their journey. And no matter what might happen—or who might hurt them—they will never have to know complete rejection. Amen.

Love,
Jesus

LETTER 2

As Jesus set his face to go to Jerusalem, his disciples, James and John, said: "Lord, command fire to come down from heaven and consume [the unfriendly Samaritans]." But Jesus turned and rebuked them.

Luke 9:54-56

*   *   *

West of Capharnaum
Border of Samaria
After supper
Same day

Dear Disciple, my Friend,

I'm glad I didn't mail my last letter. Something else came up. I want to add this to it.

James and John, the sons of Zebedee, are both good men. Glad I chose them. But they do have a fierce temper. I've tried to warn them before not to get so steamed up about things. I did it lightly: I gave them a nickname, *Boanergez* ("Sons of Thunder"). This way, I hoped they'd cut down on their "thunder" a little.

It didn't work. They haven't changed...not yet. They got so mad at the Samaritans they wanted me to duplicate Elias's display of temper. They wanted me to get dramatic: to stand solemnly with arms outstretched on top of the hill facing town...and send lightening on the discourteous folk below...burn them to a crisp. That would show them!

I have been with them so long, and they still don't understand. Love does not use power to make people behave. Love, real love, refuses to threaten, punish, or use coercion of any kind.

And I must love. That's why I was born; that's why I have set my face toward Jerusalem. Of course, my decision to love puts me at a disadvantage. The people in that village would have given us all the groceries we wanted, if I decided to show my power. They wouldn't have taken our money; they would've fawned all over us. All I'd have to do would be to snap my fingers and show them some mighty deed (like a well-aimed lightning blast consuming the back shed of the corner store!). After such a marvel, they'd have no choice but to do me favors, just because they'd be afraid of me.

I can't do that. Fear would take away their freedom. Expressions of friendliness would be but a mockery of the real thing. I have no choice; I must simply suffer their lack of hospitality.

This saddens me so much. You know how it feels. You have friends, too, who keep egging you on with phrases like "They can't do that to you!" or "Give them a piece of your mind!" Or they will say, "Threaten them with this-or-that punishment if they don't shape up" or "Get even by using a shotgun, or an eviction notice, or the lightning blast of a few well-chosen words! That'll teach them!"

You know you can't do this. You have to suffer, not only from enemies who treat you harshly, but also (and worse) from friends trying to get you to be as evil as your enemies.

Don't lower yourself by any explosion of vengeful anger. You will be tempted to "get even"...but don't. Love refuses to use force of any kind, no matter how many friends attempt to persuade you otherwise.

When I return to my Father, I'll pray for you, especially during those times when you'll want to break down the best that's in you by a decision to use violence in any form.

This will be my prayer. I've prayed it myself—for myself—tonight. I'll pray it for you when I get to heaven:

Lord God, my Father . . . look with love upon my disciples, my friends.

They have been hurt by people who have treated them unfairly. And they have friends who are advising anger. Those they are close to want them to use force to get their way.

Give them my serenity, Father. Let them feel my peace, even in their agitated state. Let them continue on their journey with only the standard of love to guide them, never with the weapons of war, or terror tactics, or threats of silent treatment.

They could get nailed to the cross for it. I will. But let them see that love is the only way, the only way to life—your life and mine. Amen.

Love,
Jesus

LETTER 3

And it came to pass, as they went on their journey, that a man said to Jesus, "I will follow you wherever you go. But Jesus said to him: "Foxes have dens and birds of the air have nests, but the Son of Man has nowhere to lay his head."

Luke 9:58

*   *   *

The hill country of Judea
Dawn
April 30

Dear Disciple, my Friend,

Heavy fog last night. Nobody had a good sleep. As a rule, the seamless garment my Mother made me has all the warmth I need. But the wind was hard and the air was damp...and it's all I can do to keep my hands on this cup of coffee.

I feel about as much like writing this letter as I do moving the boulder I'm leaning on. But maybe *because* of my discomfort, and the fact that I don't feel like doing it, maybe this is just the right time for setting down what I have to say.

It's hard to explain, when I let one thought follow another. I could say that I have no doubt about my value, and that I trust completely in God my Father. But after I said this, if I *then* mentioned how difficult it is to feel marginal among my own people and how I suffer from their nonacceptance...you might say, "Well, if you're so sure you're doing the right thing, what difference does anything else make?"

On the other hand, if I begin by saying how sad I felt yesterday, when I complained that I have no security whatever—no sure place even to lay my head!—and then I talk about my certainty that I'm doing the right thing...you might doubt the second part of my statement, too. You might say, "Well, if you're so uncomfortable about things as they are, you must have doubts about yourself, and about God, too."

But please believe me: both are present to me. I feel both of them at the same time, a real buoyancy in my heart and a real feeling of sadness.

You know how it is. You've already made some decisions that changed your lifestyle. Deep down, you know you were right to take that chance, quit that job for another one, stop associating with that person, or take on that extra responsibility, whatever it was. It was a good decision. You're more whole because of it. Your life is more full. You feel an honest pride in yourself that you didn't feel before.

Still, at the same time, you suffer from the decision. You don't have the same security you used to have. You don't have the same number of friends. There were many things, enjoyable things, you used to be able to do, and now you can't do them because you lack the time or money.

To a degree, you are "out of it." Foxes have their secure places, their snug homes; birds have their "nest eggs." You don't.

And so you suffer. You may still have a place to lay your head. But security (as the worldly spirit wants security) is beyond your reach. Responsibilities have stretched out the area of your concerns and cut down your freedom to please yourself.

You also suffer from a lack of popularity. Oh, the people in your life that really count—they love you. But you can't be a part of the social whirl the way some do; for this kind of association demands leisure time for chatting, an easy pace, familiarity with new books and movies...and ample charge cards. These aren't available to you.

Never mind. Don't be discouraged because you feel the drain, as well as the rightness, of your decision. I'll be praying for you, always, and especially when thoughts about all those things you lack in life tend to get you down.

When I'm lifted up to heaven, I'll point you out to my Father...and I'll call you my friend:

Lord God, my Father...look with love upon my disciples, my friends. Be extra kind to them when they are tempted to doubt the best decisions they ever made.

Don't let the tempter get to them...even if their choice makes them feel marginal, because they have lost some of their status and luxuries.

Don't let them throw away their own nobility. Don't let them ever think they're worthless.

Give them my sense of worth, to add to theirs. Let that be all the security they need. Amen.

Love,
Jesus

LETTER 4

[As Jesus continued on his journey] the seventy disciples returned with joy, saying: "Lord even the devils are subject to us in your name." And Jesus said to them: "I saw Satan fall like lightning from heaven. Behold, I have given you authority...over the power of the enemy; and nothing shall harm you...."

Luke 10:17-24

*   *   *

The hill country of Judea
Late evening
May 6

Dear Disciple, my Friend,

The fire's died down. All my disciples are asleep. I can't sleep. In fact, I don't care to. It's my night to keep vigil. After I write this, I'll be off to that high hill, due north of here. I need time to pray to God, my Father.

Before I do, I must tell you about my excitement. It's been a thrilling day for me—thrilling and joyful. I was alone for a couple of days, after I sent my seventy men, two by two, on their first missionary journey. They were given their pilot test. I have to start thinking of when I'll be lifted up, and leave my *Way to God* in their hands. As a lioness gives her cubs their first taste of blood so that they may grow to be hunters, I had to let my disciples have their first clash with the devil so that they'd know that they can—and must—deliver people from the power of evil.

They returned today. Oh, it was beautiful. I never saw them so happy, so sure of themselves, so glad to be with me. I was happy, too. Never felt happier. In a flash, I knew that Satan's domination was over. I saw it in a flash!

Tonight we had a party here in this desert place to celebrate the achievement. What we experienced was something like the joy that happens at the end of a war. But our joy was greater, for a greater war was won.

Now I'm dejected. Don't be surprised that I've gone from high to low so quickly. You've done it too. It's not a matter of inconsistency; it's just that one truth triggers off another truth. Both are true, but each one produces a different reaction.

So it is with me. I rejoice, as I never have before, because victory is assured. My love has triumphed over hatred and division. The work

I came to do is an assured success. My death on the cross will be a terrible ordeal, but it will be worth it. That's certain now.

But it's so long a time away. Satan's knowledge of his failure will make him all the more fierce. Once hatred knows it'll lose, it becomes more hateful and destructive.

Any time sin is aware of the crisis of a showdown, one of two things happen: either humble repentance or the arrogant hardening of its sin. With the devil, it can only be the second choice...and I must bear the full force of it! No more guesswork now. Hell, in all its fury, is out to get me. And for me, I must wade through the terrors of my last few months on earth with only this one good day to keep me going.

To some degree, you know how I feel tonight. When you've determined to start developing good habits—or to stop being controlled by bad ones—you know you're doing the right thing. There is a hunch about it, a presentiment that success will come, thanks to the order you put into your life.

But there are foes, inside yourself as well as outside, that will attack you for it. Maybe you've pledged to stop smoking or overeating, maybe to join Alcoholics Anonymous. Maybe you promised you'd pray an hour longer each day, or spend more time with your family; maybe you said a firm no to a life of sin, or to a group of companions who're dragging you down; whatever....

As soon as you sense victory, the "losers" inside your soul and outside your body will fight like mad. And you won't feel success (still in the future) nearly as much as you will feel the tugs on your nerve—and nerves—trying to win you back.

Never mind. Keep going no matter how dreadfully your devils attempt to pull you into their power. My power's greater than theirs. If you stay with me, nothing can really harm you.

And remember that I'll stay with you. I'll be for you. I'll remind my Father of the times when I also felt the fierce hatred of the adversary. And I'll pray for you this way:

Lord God, my Father...look with love upon my disciples, my friends.

Give them special love when they are discouraged by the ordeal of winning-yet-not-winning.

They are afraid, because the time it takes seems so very, very long...before they master their emotions and have success within their grasp. The devil of discouragement, bad company, and old habits of self-indulgence—all these keep trying to drag them away from their good resolve.

Let them feel joy in the success they have already tasted. Let them submit to the constancy that life demands. Let them not yield to any breakdown of the best that's in them. Amen.

Love,
Jesus

LETTER 5

And [as he continued on his journey] behold, a certain lawyer stood up to put him to the test, saying: "Teacher, what must I do to inherit eternal life?"...Then the lawyer, wishing to justify himself, said to Jesus: "And who is my neighbor?" Jesus replied: "A man was going down from Jerusalem to Jericho, and he fell among robbers...."

Luke 10:25-36

*　　　　*　　　　*

Close to the Jericho Road
Judea
After supper
May 9

Dear Disciple, my Friend,

I feel very good tonight. It's an especially good feeling because it could've turned out so bad.

I want you to have this letter so that you won't think that I'm always having heavy thoughts. (I do write, as a rule, about what I suffer. I want you to learn from my example how to handle your own trials. But even on this last journey, there are events that have something upbeat to them. I want to share these, too.)

All in all, it's been a good week. I already wrote you about the happy reunion of my disciples. They forgot their gloom of a few weeks back. They could only think of the praise due to my Father and the power of my name.

Another good thing happened today. I'm really relishing it. On the surface, it may not seem like much of an experience. After all, I've preached the good news under heavy opposition before. But this was different. Because of the way I managed this encounter, thanks to my Father, I know nothing can daunt me. There's no way that evil can get me really down.

I'm writing this letter because it's a good learning experience for both of us.

Oh, they've been coming after me for weeks on end. My enemies, always checking up on me. I can feel my cheeks and the back of my neck burn, just knowing how they watch me, and watch me... waiting for me to do something illegal so that they can report me to the authorities. They'd like nothing better than to catch me in a trap I can't squeeze out of!

Then, this afternoon, they send one of their brilliant prosecuting attorneys. He didn't want to learn the truth; he only wanted to trap me or to make a statement to convince ordinary people I was a fake.

For a moment, he made me very angry and very hurt. All I want to do is to teach God's truth and do my work of love. Why can't they leave me alone? Why can't they wait and see what I produce in the long run...without putting pressure on me with their caustic questions and their hate-burning eyes?

You know how it feels. Maybe you don't have enemies as relentless as mine, but you have some. They take away your composure; they won't leave you in peace. You could do your work so much easier, if only you didn't feel them with their "hot breath" ready to pounce on you as soon as you make a mistake. It's so frustrating at times; you feel like screaming.

That's how I felt at first. Then I thought, "Wait a second! This is a great opportunity. The best way to get people's attention is to let them eavesdrop on a conversation that doesn't directly involve them. This is especially true if the conversation is a battle of wits. (If they think they are going to watch a fight.)

"Good!" I said to myself. "All of a sudden, I have everyone's attention. Here's my chance...."

Then I told them about love and the sacrifice that love demands. You know the story well. The Parable of the Good Samaritan is one of my best!

As I think about it, the story just seemed to pour out of me. My adrenalin was really flowing. Not only were the senses of my disciples perked up; mine were, too. So that's another reason for being glad about a situation that starts out so wrong. When you get all worked up, you can sometimes work things out much better; you concentrate more.

Think of these things, my disciple, my friend, when you get stuck in similar circumstances. Be flexible. Much good can come out of a bad scene. Love can happen in the midst of hatred and enmity...if you are prepared for the possibilities. Don't just grouse and get grumpy. Turn the situation around. Use your wits and let the Spirit guide you.

Don't worry. My prayers—now, and when I get to heaven—will be with you. Prayers like this:

Lord God, my Father...look with love upon my disciples, my friends.

I don't ask that you turn their hearts to stone. When enemies gang up on them, or when fellow-workers start checking up on them, they are not supposed to like it. It hurts. That's only human. I hurt from the same kind of assaults.

But this is what I ask you, Father: don't let them resort to angry outbursts or give in to moodiness because of it. Help them use the occasions profitably. These very occasions may be challenges to test their love. They may also be opportunities for them to show love to others.

Let them come alive to the possibilities for growth. Don't let them go dead on us...or others...or on themselves. Amen.

Love,
Jesus

LETTER 6

As Jesus continued on his journey to Jerusalem, he entered a village...and a woman named Martha received him into her house. She had a sister called Mary who sat at the Lord's feet and listened to his teaching. But Martha was distracted with much serving. . . . And the Lord said to her: "Martha, Martha, you are anxious and troubled about many things; one thing is needful. Mary has chosen the good portion. . . ."

Luke 10:38-42

*   *   *

Village of Bethany, Judea
11:00 PM
May 21

Dear Disciple, my Friend,

It's very late as I write this. I've had a long day and a stimulating evening. I want to get this off to you while the experience is still fresh in my mind, the plus and the minus, the good and the bad of what went on tonight.

I've been busy helping people, curing them, preaching the good news to them. I needed to unwind. . .to just "be". . .with two of my friends. Talking to close friends is different from talking to the crowd, or even to my disciples. With them, I have to be thinking of everything: to make sure I say the right things and not too much at once. With friends like Martha and Mary, I just spill out what's in my heart.

You know how it is. You have a few special people you can let down your hair with and simply be yourself. With them, you can let the words come out just the way they will. It's good to have close friends like them, especially after weeks of working hard and being careful about what you say and do.

That's how I felt this afternoon. I didn't care what I had for supper. What I wanted to do was take off my sandals, sit in an easy chair and tell two sympathetic people how tired I feel (and how I fear the future, when I'd finally get to Jerusalem not too long from now—and be crucified). How would I handle it? Would the hatred of my enemies scandalize my disciples? Does anybody know how it hurts to realize that all the people I'm helping now won't be around to stick up for me or take my side?

I wanted to talk about these things, and I needed their support. I guess I just wanted to be assured that they cared enough to sit down and listen to me.

Mary did. Martha didn't. She was too busy, too distracted. I know she was doing it for me, but no matter what I said to her, she wanted to feel right about herself before she could relax. I told her I'd be happy with just a bowl of leftover soup and some bread. But she wouldn't allow it. She even tried to make her sister get up and fuss over the big meal, too.

It's hard when your close friends put demands on you like that. (Martha didn't realize she was putting demands on me. She was, though. She was forcing me to suppress my needs until she became quite satisfied that her need was fulfilled—her need to feel she was a better hostess than anybody in Bethany).

You have your versions of people like Martha, people who have to feel good about themselves and get everything "right" according to their own needs before they'll permit themselves—or you—to be comfortable.

No matter what you tell them, no matter how directly you express yourself that you just want a friend to listen with willing ears and a compassionate heart—they have to love you their way, instead of yours.

I'm writing you about it just to tell you that I understand the hurt (even if it's a "little hurt") when the same thing happens to you that happened to me today. Know that this is also part of the passion. You can't change certain people; you can't force them to forego their compulsions and eccentricities. You live with it. You love them patiently—and you keep going. (Remember, you aren't perfect either. You have your own eccentricities that get on other people's nerves.)

Two things I want to say before I seal this. There are both "Marthas" and "Marys" in your life. Just because some are too preoccupied to listen to you when you need them, not everybody is so consumed with self. Be glad for those who have good ears . . . and be patient with those who are too busy. Be both.

And remember, always, that I'm with you. I'm one of your "Mary friends." Like her, I'm never too busy to sit down and listen to the concerns of your heart.

Indeed, when I'm lifted up in glory, this is the prayer I'll pray to my Father . . . our Father:

Lord God, my Father . . . look with love upon my disciples, my friends.

Give them my strength when people they had hoped to get support from are too distracted by their own pursuits to take time off—who are too busy with their own bothering to bother with them.

Father, cheer them up with the presence of my Spirit. Let them talk to me. Assure them that I understand, and I want to listen...and I will, unclutteredly, be theirs. Amen.

Love,
Jesus

LETTER 7

Now [as Jesus continued on his journey] he was casting out a demon that [had made a man] dumb. ...When the demon had gone out, the dumb man spoke. And the people marveled. But some of them said, "He casts out demons by Beelzebul, the prince of demons!"

Luke 11:14-15

*   *   *

Hill country, north of Judea
Just before supper
June 1

Dear Disciple, my Friend,

Believe it or not, I wasn't planning to write about the psychological passion I endured today. I did—and I will—suffer from the malice of my enemies. They have many tricks, but just one strategy: They keep trying to ruin the good I do by mounting a whispering campaign against me. They don't bother me all that much. Not any more.

I guess I was ready for it. I expected it. Believe it or not, Martha troubled me more last week when she was too busy to listen to me. This hurt, because she's my friend. I had hoped to receive better treatment.

But the Pharisees have lost most of their power to aggravate me. They have no more surprises. I take it for granted that they'll try to turn my good deeds into mean intentions. The reason they do this is because they themselves are mean. They perform their religious duties for the sake of selfish ends. And so, they think all kindness is manipulative...as theirs is.

Today's confrontation is a case in point. I healed a man who had no power of speech. The ordinary people marveled. When I expel a devil who's made a man mute, I must be more powerful than the devil. Only God has such power. Therefore, I must be from God.

Obvious! But not to my enemies. They claim I cure maladies because I get my power from the "boss devil," Beelzebul. They accuse me of being a sorcerer who twirls people around my finger until I mesmerize them completely...and then hand them over to Satan!

Ridiculous, of course. I understand their bias. But my apostles were really shocked. They're suffering—deeply and greviously—because of my battles with all these influential people. (They grieve for themselves, too. They're being labeled as "Satan's henchmen" because of their association with me. So they're targets for the venom of the Pharisees, no less than I am.)

Because of my apostles' reaction, it occurred to me that you, too, will suffer some of your most poignant hurts for the same reason. After all, your life is linked with mine, so you, too, will be taunted by those who attack you for your faith. Some seculars and scholars will do it; the militant atheists surely will. And you'll discover that some people who don't go to church any more feel they must be defensive about it and label you a pious fraud because you do.

Besides these unsavory characters, you'll have your share of enemies who try to run a smear campaign against you for any number of reasons. They'll interpret the good you do as a ploy of pride, or a desire to be in the limelight. They will say, for instance, that you're kind to people only because you want to get on their good side so that, later on, you can manipulate them for your own selfish purposes. Things like that.

Never mind. There'll always be such people in your world. Develop a thicker skin. This is what I just told my apostles; that's what I'm telling you.

There are plenty of things in life with greater reason for causing you grief. The fact that your enemies do all they can to ruin your reputation should not be one of them. That's politics—their politics, not yours.

Don't let them get you down. Remember, I'm on your side, encouraging you. I'll continue to do so—for you, and for all who suffer like you.

When I'm with my Father, I'll look at you and notice your downcast face...and I'll pray:

Lord God, my Father...give courage and consolation to my disciples, my friends.

They hurt from the malice of their enemies. They feel they don't deserve such hatred...when they, for their part, are only trying to do good. Also, they feel the sting of those who try to destroy their faith with clever arguments and biting sarcasm.

Let them remember me, when they get down...how I suffered in the same way. The servant can't expect to be greater than the master.

Send them my Spirit who will tell them so. And give them a tougher skin toward enemies...and a softer heart toward us. Amen.

Love,

Jesus

LETTER 8

[Continuing on his journey, Jesus was preaching to the people. Just before he finished] a woman in the crowd raised her voice and said to him: "Blessed is the womb that bore you and the breasts you sucked!" But Jesus said: "Blessed, rather, are those that hear the word of God and keep it."

Luke 11:27-28

*　　　　　*　　　　　*

The other side of the Jordan
Near ruins of the ancient Moabites
After supper
June 8

Dear Disciple, my Friend,

It's been a relatively uneventful week. I've been going about doing good, preaching the kingdom, urging a change of life to all who
would hear me out. The Pharisees have been hassling me in their usual
way. The ordinary people hang on my words and push and shove for
healing....

It's been a good week, all in all. The sadness I feel is nothing
specific; can't put my finger on it. But I can't snap my fingers to take it
away, either. It just hangs there!

I know I'll suffer much worse than this. Crucifixion will be much
more painful. But perhaps because the physical passion will focus all
my energy on the actual moment, I may not feel that passion as much
as what I am feeling today.

There's no focus. All future time is placed into one draught of
bitter wine...and I must drink it until the world ends. It's the most
universal and forceless sorrow of them all. "Forceless" because I can't
do anything about it. The edicts of kings cannot change in any way
the dullness of a superficial heart. The radiant truth and beauty of
even God are impotent before the silliness of people whose minds
won't stray from their set way of thinking.

All these woeful conjectures have been sparked by an incident
that, of itself, was most inconsequential. There was a woman in the
crowd this afternoon who shouted me a blessing that the whole crowd
heard. No doubt, it was supposed to be encouraging; but it was all
wrong.

Oh, she meant well. God will bless her for blessing me. But she
didn't (or couldn't) understand what I was saying. She simply heard
me speak, and thought I was agreeable...and then thought how happy my mother must be because I grew up in such a way that would
make any mother proud.

She never heard me at all. The challenge of my words, the
revelation of God's stupendous love, the work I must do before I
triumph over evil—all this went right past her. I might as well have
been a stranger she half noticed on her bingo night, or watched on the
television soaps, or focused on for a minute or two with a couple of
neighborly gossips.

There's nothing I can do about it. My words can't penetrate the surface. I'll be forever typecast as a "nice man" who said "nice things" (to make his mother proud). She listened half-distractedly and then went off to be half-heartedly impressed by other nice things said by somebody else...and impressed by all the not-so-nice things that'll surely excite more interest in her.

For all time...for so many people...I'll be typecast this way. That woman in the crowd is representative of those who'll slouch in back of the church, so nonchalant about my love that they won't even let me feed them with my flesh. In her I can foresee all those who will make a ritual out of the 6:30 news and excuse themselves from prayer to God my Father...those who consider money and meetings more important than anything I say...those for whom Christmas is a day for the family get-together...and those for whom my Easter (the very conquering of death!) serves as the occasion for showing off new clothes. For many people, I won't be the means of their salvation; I'll only be the reason for a few holidays throughout the year!

I want to weep. I want to shake some life—real life—into the vast multitudes who only dabble, disjointedly, with the pettiness of their own immediate concerns.

The Pharisees are refreshing by comparison! Even if they're my enemies, at least I've made them thoughtful. It's the slouchers who sadden me the most, those who think they like me (as though I were "good guy Jesus"), but for all the wrong reasons. They haven't understood my claim. Either I'm the worst blasphemer in the world, or else I'm exactly what I say I am: God's only Son, and the only means of rescue for all humankind.

Pardon me for going on like this. I have to get these things off my chest. Tonight, I have to believe you'll take this letter seriously (and read between the lines) so I can revive my hope that there are individuals who'll be more than superficial in their understanding of me.

You know what I mean. In your own modest way, you've been hurt by the outrageous inconsideration of superficial people. If they ask, "How are you," you could say, "I've got cancer and I'll die tonight," and they'll answer, "Oh, that's nice," because they didn't listen. You'll feel the sting when something so important needs to be said—and passionately needs to be understood—but friends are so preoccupied by trivia and surface platitudes, you'll wish you never brought up the subject.

When such things happen, you'll be reduced to silence. It'll hurt. Never mind. At least, don't mind it so much that you give up. Go into your silence. Know the dignity of your own depth, even though others refuse to see it in you. I see it.

Write a letter to me, the same way I'm writing to you. It helps. And know that I'm with you—I'm in my presence and in my prayer for you. I'll always be with you—in that dull throb of your incommunicable pain:

Lord God, my Father . . . pay attention to my disciples, my friends.

Nobody else seems to be able to. The best aspects of my disciples, the deepest things, the noblest thoughts . . . go unattended and unremarked.

Discouragement can set in, unless the soul is nourished by acceptance.

We know how important our disciples are. Make sure they know it, too. And even if their whole world won't, or can't, listen seriously to them . . . we can, and want to . . . and we are. Let them be sure of this. Amen.

Love,
Jesus

LETTER 9

[As he continued on his journey] Jesus said to his disciples: "I tell you, my friends, do not fear those who kill the body, and after that have no more they can do to you. . . . "I tell you, every one who acknowledges me before men, the Son of Man will also acknowledge before the angels of God; but he who denies me . . . will be denied before the angels of God."

Luke 12:4-9

*   *   *

Back in Judea
Late morning
June 9

Dear Disciple, my Friend,

I almost regret what I wrote you yesterday about the Pharisees being refreshing compared to superficial people. That idea opened up a whole flood of sadness.

Let me tell you how my thought-processes went to work: I began to wonder which kind of rejection was really worse to suffer: the relentless animosity of the Pharisees or the amiable disinterest of the superficial.

That got me thinking of other kinds of rejection...and a chain reaction of the many hurts in my past life got all churned up in my heart. (Oh, Satan was at work, all right!) Then I considered my disciples, my own hand-picked friends. Some of them will disown me, too. Grace is never automatic. It can be bartered for gain, or traded in for fear.

The Pharisees have all the power. They have a weapon that can cause my people to shake in their boots. They wield like a club the threat of exclusion. All they have to do is point the finger of blame, and the accused is kicked out of the synagogue. This is a heavy threat, even to the irreligious. "Expelled from the synagogue" means more than excluded from religious worship. It means ejected from society and all the benefits tied in with it. People who acknowledge me won't be able to pray with their family, sell property, or even go to the market for shopping. They'll be ostracized; they'll be "social lepers."

Some won't be able to endure such punishment. That's what Satan tried to warn me about when he tempted me in the desert. The world's run by control, not by love.

Yet I must love. I must not allow myself or any of my disciples to use control. This makes me a person who is not "with it." That's why some disciples who want so much to be "with it" will go without me. I'll miss them. That is my passion.

You've felt the same. The consequence of your best decisions are prompted by love. You need much courage to stand by these decisions. Your enemies will hate you for it. (you show them up.) At the very least, they'll jeer you and make fun of your ideals. You'll be flaunted for being my disciple.

Then some of your friends will fear the flaunting. They'll realize that they've become less socially acceptable because they're associated with you. They'll disown you. Some already have. This hurts.

Never mind. Love, real love, is proven by courage and patient endurance. Your greatest sorrows will come when you painfully watch fair-weather friends show you their backs as soon as your friendship forces them to make sacrifices.

Be with me, especially when you're being disowned, betrayed, or suddenly stranded. I'll be with you. I always have been. These are the times I'll be with you most of all. Even in your pain, try to feel the spirit of my prayer for you:

Lord God, my Father . . . look with love upon my disciples, my friends.

They are friends. I know it now, for they keep my law of love even as they are rejected.

It's hard for humans to be still, hard for them not to quit . . . when so many of their friends are going over to the other side.

They want life to be easy and secure, just like everybody else. They don't always want to be battling against the way the world does things. They know the power they could have, if only they gave vent to angry outbursts or threats of silent treatment.

But they refuse such shabby weapons. Their way is one of patience, love, and trust. And so they sometimes feel marginal.

When they are in such straits, let them go to the friends they still have, and come to us—and come to know what friends are for. Amen.

Love,
Jesus

LETTER 10

[As Jesus continued on his journey] one of the multitudes said to him, "Teacher, tell my brother to divide the inheritance with me." But Jesus said to him, "Man, who appointed me a judge or arbitrator for you?" And he said to all, "Take heed and beware of all covetousness; for a man's life does not consist in the abundance of possessions."

Luke 12:13-21

*　　　　　*　　　　　*

Galilee
Near the brownstone caves
Early evening
June 16

Dear Disciple, my Friend,

Supper's just finished. My disciples are cleaning up. They're really good men. Without my saying anything, they knew I wanted to be left alone for a while. I have to think things out and spend time, much time in prayer to my Father.

It hit me again today; it laid such a load of sorrow on me. I probably wouldn't have even paid attention—it would not have mattered much—if I were not going to Jerusalem to be lifted up.

But I am going. And I wonder what my work will mean. Will all I do make any difference to anybody? That young man who interrupted me this afternoon, wanting me to give him leverage in his family quarrel about money, he's like the woman I met a few days ago. Both represent so many millions of people who'll come after them.

The woman was only superficial, but this man was mean and manipulative. He didn't listen to me. It meant nothing that I challenged him to have a change of heart, to stop being so selfish and money-grubbing, to shape up and turn his life to one of loving service. All my teaching flew right past him. He was looking out only for himself. He wanted to use me; he wanted to change the heart of somebody else, so he could be richer and happier. He didn't want to change, only to change his brother.

You know how it feels to suffer like this, to be exploited by friends and acquaintances. They don't care about you or about any real relationship with you. They just want to use you: to get more money for themselves, or have an audience so that they can air their gripes, or get you to be on their side in their never-ending family squabbles!

They want you to do something for them so that they can make other people more pliable to their selfish wishes.

Never mind. You can't change them. They'll always think everybody else should change, never themselves. Keep going, despite the pain you feel when you want to be loved and listened to . . . yet are only thought of as "useful," a broker for other people's self-interests.

You can't get through to them any more than I could. But you can get through to me. I'm asking you to let me get through to your heart, too. Then you'll hear the prayer I pray to God my Father for you:

Lord God, my Father . . . look with love upon my disciples, my friends.

They sometimes feel unwanted as a person, because so many people want them only for their service. They are only "functions" to serve other people's selfish ends.

It's hard to live like this. They feel like quitting sometimes. Quitting on everybody, even on us. "What's the use?" they say.

Show them Father, by the Spirit of my presence, that we love them. You sent me to tell them so. I journeyed to Jerusalem to show them. We are different from people who try to use them.

Let them understand that not everyone is selfish. Help them to be a bit more easy on the world around them, and a lot more easy on those who are true friends—who are not manipulative . . . like us. Amen.

Love,
Jesus

LETTER 11

[As Jesus continued on his journey] he said, "Do not be anxious about . . . what you shall eat or what you shall wear . . . . Which of you, by worrying about it, can add six inches to his stature? If, then, you are not able to do so small a thing as that, why are you anxious about the rest?"

Luke 12:22-26

Barren sand dunes
East of the Jordan
After lunch
July 4

Dear Disciple, my Friend,

"So small a thing," "so small a thing." I said it again yesterday. It seems that smallness and pettiness are getting to me these days. Maybe the heat has something to do with it. And the desert places we have set our tents in.

So many people are all upset over things that are of no more account than these grains of sand I hold in my hand. I'm tempted to wonder if people are all the same—stretching out for all eternity, as far as the eye can see. Is it to be forever a matter of worrying about money, jealousy over clothes, griping about the food, waiting for the paycheck and arguing about what to spend it on?

Is this what I'm sent for? Will I die on the cross to give people such wonderful things I hold out for them, only to realize they aren't reaching. . .they won't accept? They have their hands clenched, holding on to their own worries.

You know what I mean. It's happened to you, too. You want to talk to some special persons in your life. You have something important to say or something for them that'll be to their advantage. But they don't even listen to you.

It's not that they won't—they can't. They're too filled with fears. It's like trying to reach somebody on the telephone and the line is always busy. They're preoccupied, caught up with anxious concerns, disjointed by their own crushed hopes and their disappointments in the past. They keep bringing up their list of gripes about how life has treated them so unfairly.

You might as well be talking in a foreign language. They can't hear you anyway. Remember Martha, a few months back? She couldn't listen because she had to get everything right with herself before she could relax. Well, the complainers are much worse than that. They have to feel right with themselves, too. But the only way they can stop fussing about life and worrying about the future is to turn back time. . .to "do over" the situations that caused them sadness in all their yesterdays.

Martha only had to prepare a seven-course dinner. These people have to change the past, which is, of course, impossible. They fume over what was, fuss about what is, and worry that what will be is bound to be more of the same bad news.

Never mind. Don't feel bad because you feel this way. You're bound to feel bad when others (for whatever reason) won't listen to you. That's part of the passion you're going through. Love can't force anyone—and you must love—and "forceless" love will often meet rejection. The overbusy people with their agitated hearts are one cause of this rejection.

You can't do a thing about it, so let it hurt. But don't let it stop you from loving.

It's not stopping me, and I won't stop you, either. I'll see to it. When I'm lifted up to heaven, I'll send you my Spirit. When the Spirit comes, you'll be able to feel bad about rejection and persevere in love—both at the same time.

This is the prayer I'll pray for you to God my Father: (Just make sure your own head is not busy with worry. Then you'll be able to hear me clearly.)

Lord God, my Father...look with love upon my disciples, my friends.

They sometimes don't know where to turn. They get so down, so deeply down, when good things don't seem to show up. They get depressed by the company of despondent people— those who find such constant fault with fretful things, and bellyache about what's wrong, and have no heart to live...no ears to listen.

Let my disciples part company from these people, now and then. Let them find a quiet space, where hope can happen. There, let them turn to us. See to it that they give us permission to give them our encouragement...and our courage. Amen.

Love,
Jesus

LETTER 12

[As Jesus continued on his journey] he said: "Let your loins be girded [make sure you are wearing your work clothes] and your lamps burning, and be like men who are waiting for their master to come home. . . . Blessed are those servants whom the master finds awake. . . . He will put on his apron and have them sit at table and he will come and serve them."

Luke 12:35-38

* * *

Tentsite, east of Carmel
Just after supper
July 18

Dear Disciple, my Friend,

We had a delicious meal tonight. Andrew cooked it. They all take turns. Some are better than others. Andrew's the best.

I think, the meal was memorable also because there were no squabbles or petty jealousies about who was sitting next to me or who was monopolizing the conversation or who was doing more work than the others.

This afternoon, they heard me warn them against getting lazy or complacent. It's so easy to get this way, even for good people. My apostles are all good men, but they need a jolt every once in a while.

So do you. The "work clothes" I talked about, and the "stay awake" and the "keep the lights on"—these words are symbols, of course. They say, "Concentrate on serving others; don't think so much about being served by others."

I don't mean you shouldn't have your rest or enjoy yourself from time to time. I just did this very night. I had a most enjoyable supper, shared with friends.

The work I refer to is the work of service and compassion. You can't start thinking that other people exist to take care of you. If you start "expecting things from others," it won't be long before you drop into the pit of depression. You'll get angry at those who don't fulfill your needs. You'll begin to nag, telling others "It's not fair!" when you get stuck with responsibilities that they've managed to dodge.

Watch out for those words, "It's not fair!" People who say that kill their faith. When your life on earth is over, if you have persevered, I'll put on the apron and serve you. But until then, you have the apron and you better use it. You're to love others, even when they don't love you—even when they let you do most of the chores.

Don't worry. I know the good you're doing. I appreciate it. Wait for my rewards...and for the time that I see fit to give you these rewards.

But having said that, I want to balance my warning with some consolation. Believe me, I know how disturbing it can be to get stuck with an overload of work...when other people are too busy to notice that you need cooperation, or are too lazy to bother.

I felt it, too. It's discouraging to be put into a "no-help situation." I know it hurts; that's why I brought up the subject.

It's okay to feel bad when you are somehow forced to shoulder more than your share. (I'm speaking about some of your situations at home or on the job, or taking care of aging parents, or doing without, because spendthrifts throw money away...things like that.)

It's okay to be hurt by such things. But it's not okay to forget my teaching about the "work clothes," the lesson I taught my disciples this afternoon. And it's not okay to forget my example of loving service for you...or my insistence that deep down I am the only one you need. I know what's going on when you're "put upon"; I appreciate you for what you're doing.

Please remember that I suffer with you when you are burdened with more than your fair share of work. Please remember. Otherwise, you'll turn into a chronic griper yourself.

When I'm lifted up, this will be my prayer to God my Father...especially when the shirkers of your world drain your enthusiasm and sap your strength:

Lord God, my Father...look with love upon my disciples, my friends.

They are unfairly treated sometimes. They are expected to give more time, more energy, than other people. But the duties and the drudgery are the inside stuff around which love is wrapped. So somebody has to do it.

Promise them, Father, that I will do all I can to inspire the lazy ones to take more responsibility and share the work load. But I can't force anyone—they know that. So sometimes they'll be stuck.

Even so let them continue their work of love. It can't last forever.

Heaven is the only place that has forever. And I will be in

heaven as soon as their forever starts . . . and I will sit them down at a place of honor, and I will wait on them. Amen.

Love,
Jesus

LETTER 13

[As Jesus continued on his journey] he said: "If the servant says to himself 'My master is delayed in coming'; and he begins to beat the menservants and the maidservants, and to eat and drink and get drunk. . . . The master of that servant will come on a day when he does not expect him and at an hour he does not know, and will punish him."

Luke 12:45-46

*   *   *

Tent site, east of
Carmel
Early morning
July 19

Dear Disciple, my Friend,

I've more to say about what I said last night, but I wanted to write two different letters, so you can pray over this at a different time. Enough, for one day, to digest my warning about laziness and my reminder that I feel it, too, when you suffer from the shirkers of your world.

But this is something else, and the suffering goes deeper. Almost every family has its feuding members. Almost every person can tell a story of grief because someone is a prisoner of drink, or drugs, or gambling, or some compulsion.

Probably you have a tale of grief, too. If not now, you've had one or will have. Nothing you can do about it. Feuds will continue, no matter how you try to patch things up. Sometimes for years on end (maybe for life), the bottles or the needle will have more power over your loved ones than anything you can say or do for them.

This hurts...it has to. It hurts me also. It's hard enough to be rejected by other people's laziness; it's much worse to be rejected by somebody's obsession. It's also much worse when friends or family prefer to fight with one another than even notice (much less care) that you're torn apart by their mean-heartedness.

I know how it feels. I grieve as you grieve. But you must continue and do your work of love. Sometimes you can patch things up. Keep hoping, praying, and thinking of new approaches. Sometimes you can reach the addicts so that they'll move themselves to seek help and wrestle free from what is keeping them in chains.

But whether you're successful or not, you have to keep trying. Don't give up. If you do, you'll soon give up on yourself...and then on us.

Every rejection of your love is a rejection of love itself. And I am love. For centuries, I will feel the full brunt of all who would rather beat up on people or on themselves than be patient with life's delays. You're hurt by only a few of them, but I'm hurt by the rejection of them all.

I don't say this to belittle your sorrows or to make light of you. I say it only to remind you of my com-passion. I know what you're going through; I experience the same helplessness.

I had to continue even though I was aware that so many of my disciples will end up the way I predicted yesterday afternoon. It hasn't stopped me from loving them. I'll still love them, even to the cross.

I urge you also (indeed, I command you) to do the same. Don't worry, I'll be with you. This is my prayer for you when you think hopelessness is all there is:

Lord God, my Father...look with love upon my disciples, my friends.

They're troubled because they don't seem to be getting anywhere. No matter what they do, they cannot stop someone they love from giving in to the frenzy of compulsiveness.

Because they aren't successful, they are beginning to doubt themselves. Don't let them do that, Father. Cheer them up.

Remind them that I wasn't all that successful, either. Love, when it's real love, does a lot of losing. Let them remember the passion of my helplessness...and also my compassion of their own. Amen.

Love,
Jesus

LETTER 14

[As Jesus continued on his journey] he said: "The servant who knew his master's will, but did not...act according to his will, shall receive a severe beating....Everyone to whom much is given, of him much will be required; and of him to whom men commit much, they will demand the more."

Luke 12:47-48

*   *   *

Nazareth
Mid-morning
August 1

Dear Disciple, my Friend,

A break in the routine. Yesterday, I sent my disciples home for a couple of days. I wanted a break, too. I wanted to see my mother and talk over some things that have been puzzling me. I wanted to know how she's coping with loneliness now that she is by herself. Other things, too, that I can't go into.

Just one night in my own bed and I'm feeling better. Early this morning I took a long walk around the countryside. Everything is growing so beautifully. Vines and trees are bursting with fruit. Fields are rich with grain. I especially enjoyed passing by those fields and vineyards that Joseph and I used to work as hired hands. Good memories came back.

Yet there was a tinge of sadness to it. I was much more successful those days than I am now, as Messiah of my people. I'd plant my garden in the back, work in the shed fixing furniture, or sow grain in a neighbor's meadow, and it would all turn out well. There was satisfaction about it. Now, though, I'm working much, much harder...and the results I see are much more meager. Human obstinacy and laziness are not as easy to work with as the soil of the receiving earth.

Even my disciples...so much has been given them by my presence and patient teaching. And some of them will squander it away. Already, some of my Seventy have left me. I'm not even sure of the allegiance of my twelve apostles—not all of them. I've warned them not to fritter away their talents, not to take lightly the good education I'm giving them, or the rich possibilities of life I'm offering.

But some of them have done just that, and countless multitudes after them will do the same. They'll spurn my gifts, make light of their calling by God, misuse their energies by sulking and selfishness. The good wheat I've sown in hearts will come to nothing but barren briars. No fruit.

You know how it feels. You can't do anything about it, either. It'll happen to a friend or a member of your family. Often, the most talented—those for whom so much time was spent in cultivating their gifts—they are the ones who squander themselves most casually. Free will is a mysterious thing. Judas Iscariot's the best educated and most gifted of all my apostles....I'm especially concerned about him.

Never mind. I must continue to love. I can't give up on anybody, even though some give up on me (and on themselves). There is more I can do; there are more incentives I can suggest when I see them again. I have to keep going...to keep loving...to keep trying to be as good a farmer of human growth as I used to be of vegetables.

You, too. Same thing. Same way. No matter how discouraged you are, prepare yourself to persevere in hope. I'll be with you in all the let-downs of your trying times:

Lord God, my Father...look with love upon my disciples, my friends.

I pray for them—not only for priests, parents, educators, and counselors of every kind—but for all people who care about their friends.

They hurt, sometimes, when they see such a waste of talent in the ones they love. So much could be done...if only the shiftlessness could be shaken out of them...if only they had more confidence in themselves.

But patience, only patience. Father, give those who care for others the spirit of my patience. Inspire them to try still another way to reach the squanderers.

And if they aren't successful, even then...let them reach us—to be reminded that nothing of their futile attempts is really wasted. As long as they have loved, whether the results are weeds or wheat, love has been registered by love: our love for them. Amen.

Love,

Jesus

LETTER 15

[As Jesus continued on his journey] there were some present who told him of the Galileans [who were massacred by Pilate's soldiers]. He answered them: "Do you think that these Galileans were worse sinners...because they suffered thus? I tell you, no! But unless you repent, you will likewise perish. Or those eighteen people upon whom the tower of Siloam fell and killed them, do you think that they were worse offenders than the others who dwelt in Jerusalem? I tell you, no! But unless you repent, you will likewise perish."

Luke 13:1-5

*   *   *

Outskirts of Capharnaum
Late evening
August 2

Dear Disciple, my Friend,

My mini-vacation's over. Right back into the thick of it again. My apostles spent the time fishing. They look relaxed, high-spirited again. I met them at Peter and Andrew's house. We hardly left town when we drew a crowd.

This was a good day for the most part. As long as I was healing and blessing children, I was unmolested. But as soon as I started preaching about a change of heart and repentance from selfishness, I got all kinds of flack.

It's something like the distraction that the young man tried to cause a few weeks ago, wanting me to make his brother do right by him and share the inheritance. Only this is more grand-scale. Today the crowd wanted me to express my indignation over all kinds of injustices.

They wanted me to criticize the police brutality of the Roman Empire, especially to comment about the recent scandal when 20 people were murdered in a synagogue in Galilee. They also wanted me to get on a stump and scream outrage about the latest disaster in Jerusalem. (Now I know as well as they do that it was graft that caused the tragedy. Civil officials teamed up with the construction workers to use cheap material when they built that tower, and they pocketed the difference. That's why the structure was so weak that it toppled over, killing innocent people).

Certainly such things are wrong, but I'll not be tricked into ranting against all social injustices. That's a favorite dodge. It always has been and always will be. When people don't want to look at the inperfections within themselves (the beam that is lodged in their own eye) they start joining the choruses of indignation about what's wrong with other people, especially what's wrong with the most flagrant abusers of public trust. As long as they make war against the evil in the world, they don't have to battle the evil within themselves.

You know how it feels to listen helplessly as hypocrites protest over some pet peeve. Their own house is in a mess, yet they're champions of righteousness in every area but the one that needs to be fixed up first.

There's not much you can do about it. Suffer it; that's all I could do. I kept trying to pull people back into themselves. I wanted them to redirect some of their indignation so that it would shake up the smug complacency of their own arrogance. I wasn't very successful.

You won't be, either. Never mind. All you can do is try. You very well may have to admit your lack of success. But don't get trapped into becoming indignant against the indignant ones. You can easily slide right into the mood of people who are angry all the time. Be careful of this.

I'll be praying that you may resist the rigidity of protest:

Lord God, my Father...look with love upon my disciples, my friends.

They get into a bind, sometimes. They know it is right—I urged them to it—to work for social justice and to protest cruelty and exploitation whenever it occurs. I bless them for their work in healing social evils.

But balance, Father...give them balance. Don't let them get so caught up in their causes that they forget to pray, or neglect the need to subdue all of their own self-serving ways.

Don't let them become embittered when all they hear, all around them, are causes of unrest and cries of outrage.

Give them the calm, Father, of the last words of the prayer I taught them. You will deliver them from evil...as long as they keep working against the evil in themselves. Amen.

Love,
Jesus

LETTER 16

[As Jesus continued toward Jerusalem] he told this parable: "A man had a fig tree...and came seeking fruit on it, and found none. And he said to the vinedresser, "Look, these three years I have come seeking fruit on this fig tree, and I find none. Cut it down; why should it use up the ground!" The vinedresser answered, "Let it alone, sir...until I dig around it and put on manure. And if it bears fruit next year, well and good. But if not...we will cut it down."

Luke 13:6-9

*   *   *

Town park, Capharnaum
Lunchtime
August 3

Dear Disciple, my Friend,

I'm taking the afternoon off. I can't talk to the people. They all went home. No sense trying to strike up a conversation with my apostles, either. They're also terribly upset over what I said this morning.

For months I've been telling them about the kindness of my Father. He's not a severe autocrat without compassion for human weakness. He wants us to grow, and wants to help us grow.

Just an hour ago I spoke of him as if he were ordering me to "cut down" everybody who's not producing good deeds, not bearing fruit.

I seemed to be the gentle one, willing to work with people, trying to change their hearts—no matter how slim the results. He seemed to be the angry one, tired of the lack of response he gets and regretful that he sent me in the first place.

That was their immediate interpretation. They thought it was a "family argument," a clash between the disgusted Father and the patient Son, pleading for more time.

Not so. Not at all. I'm consistent when I speak of my Father in terms of mercy, compassion, loving-kindness. The "clash" lies within my own soul. There's a conflict between part of myself against the other part.

My patient side won over my angry side. But the victory wasn't achieved without struggle. Sometimes my feelings want to direct my actions into an outburst of great annoyance. I've tried, for so long, to get people to be different: to be more kind and less closed, more thoughtful of God and others, less selfish and disgruntled with their life.

I haven't accomplished much. Oh, they marvel at my healings and are impressed with my words, but nothing lasts. A day goes by, and just like that...I'm like yesterday's newspaper. They're caught up by more anxieties and distracted by their own immediate concerns. My words aren't pursued; my love's really not accepted. There are, for the most part, no figs on the fig tree.

You know what I'm going through. You can identify with me. You try and try to help those you love. You've tried for years. Nothing happens. Their attitudes don't change. It might be their attitude toward religion...or their compulsive anger...or their refusal to be anything but selfish. Everyone has something like this. It's hardest to take when they're family...and when it's gone on for a long time.

You feel the same way I feel today. Part of you feels this way, the angry side of you. It's tempting to give in to frustration. You have your own words for it: "What's the use!" or "I can't put up with it any longer!"...something like that. Whatever the expression, you'll declare an end to your attempts. You'll say: "I cut myself off from those I'm concerned about. Why should I continue, when they never seem to change!"

Don't let this side of you get control. Recognize it as a temptation, a test. It's your passion, as well as mine, to suffer frustration after you've worked so hard and have so little to show for it.

Do what I did, when I dialogued with the two sides of myself. And make sure you allow the patient side to have the last word...so that you say, "Let's try a little longer to cultivate their hearts and care for them with practical concern—and never say die."

That can be your prayer. A good prayer. Meanwhile, in the presence of my Father, I pray for you, too:

Lord God, my Father...look with love upon my disciples, my friends.

They get so frustrated, at times...so close to the end of their rope. Try as they might, work as hard as they can, their efforts to help some people come to nothing.
See to it that they don't stop trying. Let them be patient. Discover for them a different approach....

And let them remember me—the suffering, like their own, that I went through. Give them heart so that they may take heart. Make sure they never cut down the ones they love, or cut themselves off from hope...or from the source of hope: ourselves. Amen.

Love,
Jesus

LETTER 17

[As he continued on his journey] Jesus was teaching in a synagogue. And behold, there was a woman who for eighteen years had been possessed by a spirit that left her enfeebled; she was bent over double and quite unable to stand upright. When Jesus saw her...he said, "Woman, you are delivered from this infirmity." The synagogue official was indignant because Jesus had healed on the sabbath...But the Lord answered him: "This woman, whom Satan has bound for these eighteen years, ought not she be loosed from this bond?"

Luke 13:10-17

*   *   *

Near the
Capharnaum-
    Nazareth Road
After lunch
August 12

Dear Disciple, my Friend,

We all needed a long siesta this afternoon. Phillip suggested it. I agreed. It's been quite a hot spell. We're thankful for these few shade trees to sit under.

Maybe it was the weather that made the synagogue official so spiteful. Just because it was the sabbath, he wanted to forbid me to heal a poor old woman who has been bent way over for eighteen years. Eighteen years—never able to see the stars or watch a sunset!

I knew her personally. Nazareth's not very far away. We've chatted many times. The first time I met her was about sixteen years ago. Joseph was still alive; he introduced her to me. Oh, how my heart went out to her. I've prayed and prayed that my Father would heal her infirmity. It never happened.

I could do nothing. I had no healing power in my teens and twenties. My work on earth is to be the Messiah of the Jews and redeemer of all. I must be one with the people. Only when the right time came was I given the power to establish my credentials. I couldn't be a flashy wonder-worker. God is the God of love, and love cannot intimidate anyone. Miracles by a teenager would amaze many individuals to the point of being intimidated.

So I had to wait all these years until God my Father told me to begin my ministry. And finally—after eighteen years!—I was able to help the poor woman . . . and that character in the synagogue tried to sour it on me.

You can understand my feelings. Either you or someone you know has gone through a similar experience. You've waited and waited, years and years on end, for a cure. Someone you know and love is sick. It could be a physical handicap such as my neighbor had, an emotional disability or something else that enfeebles the individual. You've prayed, and nothing happens. My Father's ways are mysterious. Why some are cured, and some remain uncured . . . I cannot fully understand myself.

This much I do understand. Free will is always at stake. My Father won't force anyone. My Father loves with a higher, greater love than people have. It's a love that knows the future, including the destiny of happiness in heaven. So divine love can be much more patient than a mere eighteen years.

I understand this, too. I know what you go through when your prayers aren't answered. I can only say, be patient. Consider my case: After all those years of waiting, the healing happened.

So perhaps with you. After four years of praying, a cure may be right around the corner. Whether it is or not, you still have to care, hope, and pray. You suffer from the state of "no change." This is part of your passion.

Another part of suffering will be this: When a cure does come, there may be some characters who'll try to take away your joy over it. They'll call you a fool for having wasted so much time and effort on that person (or they might word it, "that no-good-bum!") They might try to convince you never to forgive such a person for having caused you such grief.

Never mind the snide remarks. If health's come back to someone you love, be joyful about it; know that I share your joy. Don't bother with the "Pharisees" in your life. They'll always be the same . . . .

Time's up. My siesta's over. Back to work. I beg you not to forget that your heart is linked with mine. We're in it together, you and I. I'm praying for you, and with you all the time:

Lord God, my Father...look with love upon my disciples, my friends.

They get so demoralized, at times. There are people they care so much about—as much as I cared for my neighbor who was unable to look up.

They do not know the future as we do. They do not know your plan of grace, or the ultimate dimension of your full love. They only know the sameness of frustration, and the apparent fruitlessness of their 'unheard' prayers.

I do not ask you, Father, to hurry up the time of healing. That's your decision. I only ask that you give them the spirit of my patience, and my unfailing love for them.

Help them to remember ultimates. And then the years won't be so desperate...their waiting time won't seem so long. Amen.

Love,
Jesus

LETTER 18

Jesus passed on through towns and villages, teaching and making his way towards Jerusalem. And someone said to him, "Lord, will those who are saved be few?" And he said to them, "Strive to enter by the narrow door. For many, I tell you, will seek to enter and will not be able to."

Luke 13:22-23

*   *   *

West shore of Lake Galilee
After supper
August 14

Dear Disciple, my Friend,

Well, I did it now. I'm certain to be hung on the cross. Only a matter of time. I spoke of effort today...in a way I never did before. "Strive!" I said. The prize of perfect happiness with my Father isn't an easy thing to catch.

The people—even my own disciples—keep wanting me to make it easy for them. They want me to be a kind of global "Quartermaster Corps," feeding them with miracles of bread and fish every time they're hungry. They want me to be a popular hero, throwing off the yoke of the Roman Empire so that they can be on top of things, and strut around in palaces and live without a worry in the world.

They see now that I'm not doing it. I'm not fanning their hatred and predjudices by leading a political revolt. I'm suffering unpleasant people as patiently as I can. I live a life of service: healing and teaching and asking for no money...and it isn't easy.

Now they're frightened; they panicked. The first to panic were the ordinary people. Then my apostles. I haven't met their expectations. The personal demands I put on them are finally sinking in. The route I take is a tough one; a journey to Jerusalem and to the cross is awaiting me.

They must love as I love, without any thought of gain. This is a demanding program. They understand it now. They want me to give them rewards. Instead, I lay service on them. It was self-pity—self-pity and uneasy fear—that pushed that question up from their hearts: "After following you and obeying your instructions, will only a few be saved?"

Those were the words I heard. But I could also read their faces...and I could sense what they didn't dare to utter: "We hoped you would make things nice for us. We figured that all we had to do was give allegiance to your cause, and then we could use your power like a large down-payment...to make investments in whatever course we wanted to pursue. But now you talk about the narow door and use hard verbs like strive...and we are scared. Once the Messiah came, we thought things would be easy. You're making it tougher. Woe is us!"

When I saw their faces and felt their fear, that's when I came on strong. Some may think it was too strong. I know my words will be taken out of context and used by every bigoted group of fanatics who'll think they're the chosen ones (who have the only key to that "narrow door")...and everyone outside their little clique is damned. Even though my words will be misapplied, I had to be forceful against the instinct of self-pity. People must come to terms about me. I'm not a pushover. I won't be a "mascot" to any man or woman.

You know my feelings tonight. People have expected you to do the miraculous, to lead them to some kind of earthly paradise where they will be served to their hearts' content. You can't do this. And so they fill up with self-pity, and get "the sulks." Their teary eyes tell you how you let them down, and then they get fearful about the demands you lay on them. They want to quit on you...and maybe they do.

Never mind. Be hurt. You can't help being hurt. But don't quit on yourself, even though others may. You have me as a model. You have my grace. Your verb is "strive." Love without hope for gain; live without dominating anybody. Live a life of service, but make sure you don't let others turn you into their doormat. Above all, don't get in the habit of feeling sorry for yourself.

I'll be with you. Not just by my example and my grace. I'll be a comfort to you...for you will know by these letters that I've gone through the same distresses you have. And I'll be a prayer for you, as well as a comfort. When I'm lifted up to heaven, this'll be my part in your passion:

Lord God, my Father...look with love upon my disciples, my friends.

They sometimes can't live up to other people's expectations...and so they are wrongfully left out. But they could not in conscience meet those demands. To do so, they would have to surrender us and the best that is in them.
But they hurt just the same. Loneliness and desertion always hurts. Don't let them be infected by the virus of self-pity or by fear. Give to their journey, through their narrow door, the spirit of my journey to Jerusalem.

And be with them, loving Father, as you always were with me. Amen.

Love,
Jesus

LETTER 19

[As he continued on his journey] Jesus said: "When once the householder...has shut the door, [some of you] will begin to stand outside and to knock on the door, saying, 'Lord, open to us.' He will answer, 'I do not know where you are from.' "Then you will begin to say, 'We ate and drank in your presence; you taught in our streets.' But he will say, 'I tell you, I do not know where you come from; depart from me, you workers of iniquity!' "

Luke 13:25-28

*　　　　　*　　　　　*

Above Lake Galilee
Late evening
August 15

Dear Disciple, my Friend.

I miss my mother tonight. I'd love to be able to sit on the back porch—just the two of us—and talk about prayer, and gratitude to God, and about my concern over the hostility of the Pharisees and how it is alarming so many.

But I can't go home. Too much to do. And only a few months left before I end my course.

A change has come over the world I live in. Even my closest friends are mystified. They feel it, too—the empty places where there used to be multitudes; the gloom on the faces of those who still stay to listen to me. They used to applaud, but now they are quite uncomfortable.

It began yesterday with my "showdown" speech. And today, I certainly didn't make it any easier! I've warned them before. This time it sank in because of how I said it. I had to tell them that the people God will praise are not those who just listen to my words, or get themselves cured, or eat and drink with me...or shake my hand. My real friends are those who put my teaching into practice. Nodding acquaintance is not enough. I'm not some cheap politician who has to give them favors just because they brought in a couple of votes for me, or attended a rally once, or put ten dollars in the Christmas collection.

I demand the hard work of loving service. My true disciples must persevere, even when it's difficult to do so. They must submit to all the challenges my words convey.

That's why the crowds have slimmed down. People are leaving me in droves. They used to think that when death came they could just slap me on the back, remind me about the fine reception they gave me in Galilee some place, tell me how they introduced me to the chief magistrate in town, show me where I healed them...and I would just usher them into a favored place in the banquet hall of heaven. All they'd have to do is "mention my name" and speak of some personal anecdote and all'd be well with them for all eternity.

Not so. I told them, not so. They have a responsibility to work, constant and persevering work, for the kingdom of God. Name dropping's not enough. So the exodus has begun, and I'm left with but a few pockets of staunch friends.

You know how it hurts when it happens to you. Same thing, really. As long as you have favors to offer and service to render, you're swept along with waves of friendliness. But as soon as this turns around and you make demands on them, expecting mutual responsibility, then attitudes change. The winds of self-seeking dry up your popularity, and only a few good friends stay with you.

Never mind. My Father and I approve of the way you stick to your principles. We wouldn't have it any other way. You can't do everything yourself. There has to be cooperation, a reciprocal shouldering of the work of love.

Keep going, I beg you. Even when consolations dwindle down, stay with the best that's in you. I am with you—always will be—on the "back porch" of your quiet prayer. And when I return to heaven, I will pray for you:

Lord God, my Father...be with my disciples, my friends.

They look around, sometimes, and see a barren desert of cold shoulders where once there were smiles and open arms of gladness.

Things happen in their world, hurting things. Popularity and easy-going acceptance can't always be counted on. They decided to keep their faith in me. They confronted their friends with challenges, refusing to be pushovers.

So they are getting left out a lot lately. Ease up on them,

Father. Send them a grace, show them a sign, to make them understand that we are among the group of genuine friends.

Help them to see that even though there seems to be nobody else left, we are with them. We know how difficult it is to persevere. We are proud of them for doing so. Help them to understand this. Amen.

Love,
Jesus

LETTER 20

At that very hour [while he was on his way to Jerusalem] some Pharisees came and said to Jesus, "Get away from here, for Herod wants to kill you." And he said, to them, "Go and tell that fox: 'Behold I cast out demons and perform cures today and tomorrow, and the third day I finish my course. Nevertheless, I must go on my way...for it cannot be that a prophet should perish away from Jerusalem.' O Jerusalem, Jerusalem...How often would I have gathered your children together as a hen gathers her brood under her wings. But you would not!"

Luke 13:31-34

*   *   *

Herod's country
In the desert
Just before supper
August 20

Dear Disciple, my Friend,

Well, I scandalized more people today. Earlier this month, it was the weak ones—they didn't have the stamina, or the stomach, for my words. Now it's the courageous ones who're troubled. My apostles, especially; they saw me weeping. For a few moments, I was crying like a baby.

They were shocked by it. I see them—only about twenty yards away—getting supper ready. Long faces on them all. A few muttered words exchanged...but mostly mumbles to themselves. Half-heartedly, almost like robots, getting supper ready.

They accepted me as leader. They eagerly agreed to their discipleship. They knew I was close to God...and, by being close to me, they would be close to God, also. Well and good. But they also thought I'd set up a kingdom the way other kings do. I'd be a kind of Jewish Caesar. They have seen my control over winds and waves; they know my power to heal; they have witnessed my authority over all the powers of evil.

So they latched on to my strength and figured to wait it out until I made my move for full political power. Then they would become the "king's cabinet" and never have to suffer any more, never be poor, never again live in tents out here in the desert, as they are doing now.

They thrilled with excitement this morning when I told the Pharisees what I thought of Herod. It's the closest thing I'll ever get to a political statement. Now everybody knows what I think of that petty king, that stupid and contemptible monarch! I've no fear of him.

My apostles immediately jumped to conclusions. They thought, "Now's the time! This is it!" They were all set to raise the flag of militancy, gather up manpower as they go, sweep through Herod's territory, and on to Judea to destroy the garrisons of Rome.

Then their faces fell. I told the crowd again that I must go to Jerusalem to die. This does violence to their strategies of war. My words disarmed them.

Then—worse!—I wept. They saw how helpless I was. More than anything, I want to bring all people into my love's embrace. But I can't force anyone to believe in me. I have to wait for a free response. And it's not coming...not with my own people...not in Jerusalem. So I must perish by the hands of those I've spent my life working for.

Shouldn't I weep over this? Who wouldn't weep? If my apostles are shocked to see me crying over my helplessness, that's their problem, not mine. I never even suggested that I was a stony-hearted hero who couldn't be dismayed by adversity. They should know me by now, that when I hurt, I feel it...and when I feel it, I show it.

You know how it is. Many times in your life, you've known children, even adults, who rely too heavily on your strength. Because they're small, or scared, or weak, they demand that you be the strong one—you must be always in control. You can't let your hair down, or show your sadness, or ask them for support. They're too busy wanting you to support them. In their minds, they build you up into a ten-foot giant, with mastery over all emotions and good strategies to handle every situation.

When they see you're not that kind of hero—when they see you in your humanness—they get nervous. Then they go into their version of mumbled gloominess, as my apostles are doing to me right now. They'll try to do all they can to force you to become "strong" for them again.

Never mind. Be true to yourself. The sense of helplessness will get you down at times. And you will weep. They are good tears— honest ones. Don't be ashamed of tears.

Just remember, you have to keep going. You must love, and your love must be given without conditions...even if you perish in your version of Jerusalem. You don't go alone. My prayer and the courage of my journey are going with you:

Lord God, my Father...look with love upon my disciples, my friends.

They are burdened, sometimes overburdened, by other people's expectations.

Friends, adolescents, and little ones demand that they always be on top of things, always at their service. Sometimes they can't be all this. They suffer. They get sick. Their nerves are over-strained. They weep.

Let them know they need not be ashamed. No one can answer to others' needs all the time. Let tears refresh them. Let them be weak in our presence. We will bring strength back to them. We will teach them about true love, which sometimes grieves, but always is at peace. Amen.

Love,

Jesus

LETTER 21

One sabbath [as he was on his journey] Jesus went to dine at the house of...a Pharisee. And behold, there was a man before him who had dropsy [a painful cancer]. Jesus spoke to the lawyers and Pharisees saying, "Is it lawful to heal on the sabbath or not?" But they were silent. Then he took him and healed him and let him go. And he said to them, "Which of you, having an ass or an ox that has fallen into a well, will not immediately pull him out on a sabbath day?" And they could not reply to him.

Luke 14:1-6

*   *   *

Back in Galilee
Near the road to Jerusalem
Late evening
August 25

Dear Disciple, my Friend,

What a tiring evening. The meal was delicious. Seven courses with well-trained servants timing things just right. The cook must have been professional. Yet all that food still sits like a lump in the pit of my stomach. Give me Andrew's cooking, out in the desert, any time! When there's no love or kindness around the dining table, the meal's not nourishing...no matter how delicately prepared.

There was no kindness tonight, only malice; I could taste that more than I could taste the food. The Pharisees and their lawyers kept trying to trip me up. They threw question after question at me—tricky ones!—as though I were a candidate for their fraternity club and they were bent on proving how unacceptable I was.

Oh, it was awful...until an uninvited guest created a diversion. I was so glad the man dropped in just as we were finishing dessert. I was glad to be able to cure him of his paralyzing cancer. I was also grateful because he helped to break up the evening. The Pharisees would have kept me there forever, and I wanted to get back to my disciples.

The man gave me an opportunity to question those who were determined to keep me on the hot seat. They didn't like it. They didn't learn from it, but at least it gave me an excuse to get away.

They're certainly sticklers for the law of God, these Pharisees. "Nothing doing" on the sabbath. And they slap themselves on the back for it. "Hoorah for us; we are the defenders of God's day of rest!"

Right before them was a man—pained and paralyzed—and they were prepared to snub their brother, a child of Abraham...a son of the same God they worshipped so zealously! How can they be so mean to one of their own family?

Most of these Pharisees are prosperous farmers. They'd never treat their beasts of burden as unkindly as they wanted to treat this man. Sabbath or no sabbath, they'd get the hauling ropes and winches ...and they'd drag the beast until he was up from the ditch and out of harm and free to work again. Sabbath or no sabbath!

You know to some degree how distraught I am by the Pharisees. You know people, maybe some of your own family, who're sweetness and kindness toward strangers and toward those they work with... and even toward animals. Yet they're vicious and uncivil to members of their own family. Thoughtfulness is given for people outside the home; rigid aloofness is reserved for those who really have first claim to their consideration.

You can't do much about it. You can tell them about their two-faced behavior (as I told the Pharisees, a few hours ago), but you probably won't change them, any more than I could. They'll continue to be "street angel—house devil," as the saying goes. You'll simply have to suffer, and not grow weary of trying...and not get bitter yourself.

I can't change things for you any more than I could change things for myself. But I'll pray for you. I'll remind you that I went through it, too. And I'll give you the wisdom to see your passion linked with mine:

Lord God, my Father...look with love upon my disciples, my friends.

Some members of their family and some of their friends have a most disturbing peculiarity—they are callous toward those they should be most careful of...they are hardest on those they should be softest to.

If you can, Father—without abusing free will—change the hearts of those who have such a double standard. But if this can't be done, keep good and true the hearts of my disciples. And let them work for healing and for peace, no matter how much criticism they get.

Even if they are largely unsuccessful, the measure of their worth is how they tried, and how they lasted, despite discouragements.

Remember what I earned for them, because I lasted, even

to the cross. I have won for them the peace they're searching for: my peace, which I will give them, even in their pain. Amen.

Love,
Jesus

LETTER 22

[As he continued on his journey] Jesus said: "Whoever does not bear his own cross and come after me, cannot be my disciple. For which of you, deciding to build a tower, does not first sit down and count the cost, whether he has enough to complete it. Otherwise...when he is not able to finish, all who see it will begin to mock him."

Luke 14:24-35

* * *

Wasteland, District of Sidon
Pagan territory
Mid-afternoon
September 1

Dear Disciple, my Friend,

I was left alone most of today. Like Samaria, this place is un-friendly to us. Somebody forgot the provisions. Food prices are ex-travagant, here. The few merchants who're willing to serve Jews de-mand a high price for the "favor." So I sent my disciples back to Galilee with a large order for groceries.

I also sent them back with the request that some women join us to help with the cooking and planning. We can't be preaching all day and attending to the sick...and at the same time worry about what's for supper.

Besides, the women who are my disciples have more staying power than the men. Their faith seems to be deeper. They persevere more steadily; they're not so quick to quit.

And it's all the quitting that bothers me so much lately. I have to have some sort of nucleus...somebody to be willing to continue my work.

It's hard for people to hang on. Obstacles come up, usually in the form of boredom or some surprising discouragement. Once they bump into these obstacles, they start counting the cost. Then they discover for themselves "good reasons" for reluctance, and they leave.

The crowds who followed me have dispersed. Even the number of my disciples has thinned down. And I know (for I am going to Jerusalem) that this state of affairs is but a hint of things to come. As soon as people feel secure with themselves, my Father and I can very easily be put out of their lives. Prayer can become a lost art. The boredom that sometimes accompanies prayer is too much of a cross. Matters of the Spirit can become simply a matter of capriciousness. People will practice their religion if they "feel like it" but if they have to count the cost of perseverance (like the man in my parable) they won't stay with it.

It's sad to think how many people will decide to do their own thing, instead of following me. I'm sad thinking about it now.

You know how I feel. You may be distressed this very moment about a friend or family member who has renounced those religious principles you used to share.

There'll be many parents the world over who struggle with guilt feelings because their grown-up children have forsaken the faith... even forsaken them. If you know such parents, please show them this letter. Urge them to be patient with their family and gentle with themselves. They did what they could; they weren't always successful. I wasn't all that successful, either. I know what they're going through. Tell them so. Urge them to continue, despite discouragement. Urge yourself to do the same, if this letter applies directly to you.

But this isn't the only way you can be dismayed by people who give up on you. Like everybody else in the world, you've felt saddened when others who were once your friends are not so any longer. Your love and friendship was like a house that was half built, then left abandoned.

That hurts, I know. At such times, you'll want to give up. But don't—not on us, or others, or on yourself.

You're not alone, although many times you'll feel you are. Remember, I'm with you. Do this for me. At some time each day, close your door to the world outside and pray to our Father in secret. Wordlessly pray, in a listening mood. Then you'll hear the words I speak on your behalf:

> Lord God, my Father. . .look with love upon my disciples, my friends.
> They get upset when others give up on them. Lasting friendship, like lasting faith, puts demands on people. There is a cost to it, a cross. Some can't stick it out.
> My disciples grieve because of it. They seem to be abandoned. Whenever they are left, for whatever reason, they feel lonely.
> Please, Father, help them in their loneliness. Let them prove their faith is strong, even though it costs them.
> And comfort them in their grief, so that they may quiet down enough to know that we haven't given up on them. Then their loneliness will become something they can manage, for they will know we have included them in our everlasting love. Amen.

Love,
Jesus

LETTER 23

Now [as Jesus continued on his journey] the tax-collectors and sinners were all drawing near to hear him. And the Pharisees and their scribes murmured, saying: "This man welcomes sinners and eats with them."

Luke 15:1-2

*   *   *

Good Old Capharnaum
Late
September 29

Dear Disciple, my Friend,

Yes, "good old Capharnaum"! It hasn't changed at all. The despised elements of society have been waiting around for me. I'm not too sure they understand all I'm saying, but they are a joy to be with. They like my company and I like theirs. I can talk to them about my Father. They don't have any rigid preconceptions of how things ought to be said, or how customs ought to be observed, or what behavior fads are "in" or "out."

They've prayed the way I taught them, and they've grown in a sense of gratitude for God and for the world as it's given them. They're gracious about kindness when it comes their way. They're humble enough to know they still have work to do...and they want to learn. They admit they're sinners, and they ask forgiveness. They also thoroughly enjoy my company. I like them for that, too.

What a refreshing contrast to those rigidly righteous ones who hang around like leaches on my back. Yes, the Pharisees and their scribes still watch me. It's "good old Capharnaum," as I said. They'll get to Jerusalem ahead of me. They only murmur now. They'll be shouting later.

People afflicted with self-righteousness don't want to learn, or listen, or be receivers of God's gifts. They want to instruct others to be just like themselves (even in their eccentricities). They want to assure each other that they're the only ones worthy of approval. They can't stand anyone—they can't stand me, especially—who delights in the company of people they can't stand. In a word, they're snobs.

You know how it feels to suffer the relentless scorn of the self-righteous. If you're pleasant to somebody they disapprove of, they'll attack you with biting sarcasm or spiteful gossip.

If you suggest they listen to you...or listen to any line of reason they've not already decided on...they'll consider you impertinent. They're not interested. In fact, the only interest they have in you is the hope that you'll change into their likeness: a fellow-snob they can share their haughty mannerisms of disdain with.

Never mind. Elitism is a human scab that sometimes can't be cured. You probably won't change the attitudes of the Pharisees in your life. Just don't let them change you. Stay humble. You know how much growing in grace you must still do. Stay open to my inspirations.

Separate yourself from the clutches of those who think they know everything...and who want you to join their select club.

Delight in your friends who haven't forgotten how to be spontaneously joyful and haven't forgotten gratitude...and who're thoughtful and kind when they sit down with you to share a meal.

These are good people to associate with. And don't forget I am you companion. I want you to be like those sinners whose company I enjoyed at Capharnaum—forgiven by me, given my Spirit of life, grateful for my friendship, and easy to talk to.

If you are, it will be easy also for me to talk about you, to my Father:

Lord God, my Father...look with love upon my disciples, my friends.

They are not so confident of their own worth that sarcasm and scorn does not bother them.

They feel it when snobs attack them, by disapproving of their friends, or by throwing wet blankets on their simple joys, or by trying to put them into straight jackets of rigidity in all they think and do.

Don't let the bigots get them down. Let them be formed by us and by our law of love.

There are plenty of things in their life—real sorrows—for which they have a right to grieve. Let them not grieve over the disapproval of the disapprovers. We are the only ones from whom "getting approval" is really important. Let them remember this...remembering us. Amen.

Love,
Jesus

LETTER 24

[As he continued to Jerusalem] Jesus said to his disciples: "If you have not been faithful in unrighteous mammon [in worldly matters with no lasting consequence] who will entrust true riches to you? And if you have not been faithful in that which is another's, who will give you that which is your own? No servant can serve two masters; either he will hate the one and love the other, or he will be devoted to the one and despise the other. You cannot serve God and Mammon."

Luke 16:10-13

*   *   *

South Galilee
Abandoned farmhouse
After supper
October 2

Dear Disciple, my Friend,

The devil warned me there'd be times like this. Indirectly he did it...obliquely. Satan didn't exactly say it; he hinted it. It was when he showed me all the kingdoms of the world and all their riches. He said I'd never be lacking in supporters if I gave allegiance to "Mammon." If I wanted to get ahead in the world—to win friends and influence people—all I had to do was use his tactics and lie to people and bully them until I carved out my fortune. Then the world would be my oyster!

But I decided against being subservient to him. Exploitation by whatever tricks, manipulation in any of its forms—all these I've chosen to forego. And so I'm left with a dwindle of friends, a weakness of position, a lack of status...and a road that leads to Jerusalem and to its destined execution.

When I gave my speech this afternoon, my twelve apostles thought I was talking to them. I was. But they don't understand, not yet. They'll have to be on their own "journey to Jerusalem" before they realize that their only true possession is their own soul; the only things that are really permanent are the decisions about life and love that have fixed their attitudes and formed their values.

They'll understand this, little by little. I wanted them to hear what I said, but mostly I needed to hear it myself. I must keep alive my own comitment to the life of loving service. Mammon isn't just "money"; it's everything in the world, which of its nature can't last.

So Mammon includes almost everything. Popularity or unpopularity can't last. Both depend on other people's appraisal of you, and this is fickle. Words can't last, for words depend on a willing audience, and this likewise is fickle. I've performed many cures, and these cannot last. Even the ones I raised from the dead will die again.

My life on earth won't last. I will die too (soon now). Also, some of my close friends won't last with me; some will desert me. I can't even be certain my work will continue after I die. I can only trust my Father in this; He promised it will.

Love's as insecure as life itself. The only thing of permanence is the act of loving. All that remains in the world is the knowledge that we've been faithful to the best that was in us . . . whether we were loved in return or not, rewarded or not, made comfortable, or made to suffer all kinds of disquieting things.

Perhaps you don't understand—yet—how I feel tonight. Of course, you can identify with part of my pain. You know how you suffer when other people prove faithless to you.

But right now I'm speaking of the times when you'll wonder whether you can remain faithful to yourself. You'll ask yourself this question when you begin to face death, or when your normal lifestyle breaks down, or when a crisis stuns you into speechlessness. At such turning points in your life, you may wonder whether anything is lasting . . . whether, maybe, all of life is a farce.

Never mind. Understand these doubts to be your passion, your psychological and spiritual passion. Put memory to work; that'll be your consolation. Remember the best you've been. Remember those occasions when you were faithful, when you loved without thought of gain; when you were giving to others instead of grabbing for yourself. As long as you've been trustworthy in these impermanent concerns, you can trust the lastingness of my love for you.

And the life of this love will be your permanent possession. I'll precede you into heaven. When you arrive, this is the prayer I'll use to usher you into your permanence:

Lord God, my Father . . . look with love upon my disciples, my friends.

They have listened to my words. They have kept faith. They have followed me, as best they could.

At high cost to themselves, they risked security for the sake of service, popularity for the sake of principles, the comfort of the powerful for the care of those in need.

Reward them, Father. At last . . . at long last . . . now is the time for reward. Let them delight forever in the fullness of love and peace—in that fullness they tried to give to others, and never had enough of for themselves.

Here it is; here we are...at last. Let them relax and enjoy it. Amen.

Love,
Jesus

LETTER 25

[Continuing on his journey] Jesus told the Pharisees...who were lovers of money...this parable: "There was a rich man, who was clothed in purple and fine linens and who feasted sumptuously every day. And at the gate lay a poor man named Lazarus who desired to be fed with what fell from the rich man's table....The poor man died and was carried by the angels to Abraham's bosom. The rich man also died and was buried; and, in hell, being in torment, he said: 'Father Abraham...I beg you to send Lazarus to my five brothers, so that he may warn them, lest they also come into this place of torment.' But Abraham said: 'They have Moses and the prophets. Let them hear them.' But he said: 'No, Father Abraham; but if some one goes to them from the dead, they will repent.' Then Abraham said: 'If they do not hear Moses and the prophets, neither will they be convinced if some one should rise from the dead.' "

Luke 16:19-31

*   *   *

A caravansary
Border of Samaria
Dawn
October 7

Dear Disciple, my Friend,

It's a little after 6 AM. I slept late, but everybody else in this stopover for caravans has washed, eaten, and started off. My disciples and I are usually on the road by now. They're all ready, waiting for me. Couldn't help it. My heart was heavy yesterday. I slept like a stone, ten hours. I never did that before. The parable I told yesterday is what did it! The beginning of the story came out of my mouth just the way I planned it. I wanted to shake up the Pharisees, to scare them into being more thoughtful of the poor and less crafty with money.

The moral was simple enough. If people who have food don't notice those who don't have enough, that very act of neglect will condemn them to hell. People who want to be God's friend must be concerned about the oppressed and the poor and the deprived. This is my mandate for all forms of social justice, as it was with Moses and the prophets.

Then something came over me...I looked down the road that leads to Jerusalem. I realized what's waiting for me there. Then the whole flood of "refusals" came over me. I want to tell you about it.

The parable I told has a strong message, a stern warning, but it was as effective as a wet dishrag hurled against a castle wall! The Pharisees love money so much that they hear my words no better than they notice the conditions of the beggars in the streets.

That's the way it'll always be. I saw the whole scope of my failure...for all centuries to come. That's when Abraham "changed." All of a sudden, he became my voice. (You must understand that the "five brothers" in the parable represent all the people, for all times, who are more concerned with making money and enjoying themselves than they are with sharing what they have with those in need.) Abraham said, "They have Moses and the prophets...and they'll have my gospel. Let them learn from the written word of God."

"No!" was the reply. I heard the echo of that No! reverberating from so many people who live comfortably and consider only their own self-interest: "No, they won't take God's words seriously. Bit if someone rose from the dead...if that should happen...they would take notice and change their ways."

Then Abraham sighed. (But it was I who sighed.) Then he said, "If they don't heed the warnings in the Bible, they won't be impressed even if someone should die for them and then rise from death."

I know it now. I know that for the most part I'll be a failure. All my work and teaching...and then my passion and death...and then my resurrection—all of it will be, for so many, nothing but a waste, not even denting the defenses of selfishness.

Yet I must still go through with it, and end my course in Jerusalem. Not everybody will deny me. There'll be true disciples. I'm as sure of my success as I am of my partial failure.

I'm sure of you, too. I'm writing this letter for you, as well as for myself. I'm counting on you not to fail me.

Another reason I write to you is to comfort you when you're feeling what I feel this morning. There will be times when you too will look into the future and see all that you've worked so hard for going up in smoke. It'll seem as though all you have done and all you have been amounts to nothing.

Then the words, "What's the use in continuing," will come instinctively to mind. You'll think life has turned around and slapped you in the face...and mocked you for a fool.

Never mind. You still must love. There are and always will be people who've been helped by you. They are the ones who'll assert your value. You're not a failure. The world has become a little better because you lived in it. Be confident of this.

It's not the results that prove failure or success—if it were, I wouldn't be much of a master to follow!—it's whether or not you loved, no matter how the results turned out. My Father's the only measurer of these things, and I'm the only one who can help you continue when times get as tough for you as they are for me right now.

Here's the prayer I prayed this morning. First it was my own. I've changed it some to show you how it'll be my prayer for you when I'm with our Father:

Lord God, my Father...look with love upon my disciples, my friends.

The sometimes have a sense of failure about what they worked so hard to build. This can be a frightening experience.

I felt that way, too...as you remember. You kept me going, Father. In no way could I have stayed true to your plan of love if you didn't support me.

Support them, in the same way, for my sake. And for their sake, too. Despite surrenders on all sides, stay with them and stay them firm...so that they may finally understand success...the way we do. Amen.

Love,
Jesus

LETTER 26

[As he continued on his journey] the apostles said to the Lord: "Increase our faith." And the Lord said: "If you had faith...you could say to this sycamine tree, 'Be rooted up!' and it would obey you." [Then he observed:] "If you had a servant plowing or tending sheep, would you say to him, when he has come in from the field: 'Come at once and sit at table'? Would you not say to him, instead: 'Prepare supper for me, and put on your apron and serve me till I eat and drink; and afterward you shall eat and drink.' Does the master thank his servant because he did what was commanded? So you also, when you have done all that is commanded you, say: 'We are unworthy servants; we have only done what was our duty.' "

Luke 17:5-10

*   *   *

Somewhere in Judea
After supper
November 10

Dear Disciple, my Friend,

As you see, it's been quite a few weeks since I've written to you. The fact is, my last big battle with discouragement left me somewhat drained. I was too weary to write. (Besides, I've had much to do. I am pressed for time, so I'm devoting most of each day teaching my disciples.)

I want to write you about what went on today. It'll be written in the gospel. I told my twelve to make sure it doesn't get neglected. But I want to write you this, ahead of time, because it's so very important.

The lesson has to do with the most compelling sin that good people are tempted to commit. I'm talking about good people, like my disciples...like you. It's a particular form of self-pity. It's dangerous because it destroys faith.

My apostles touched on the subject when they asked me to increase their faith. They see that I can work more cures and do greater miracles than they can. They wanted to find out why. They wanted to improve, to grow in grace.

They'll be blessed for asking, but they should've known. I've read them every letter I wrote you. They're aware of the need for perseverance. I've repeated and repeated the necessity of struggle, the passion—that we must love even when there's not much love returned.

That's the way it'll always be. There's no "50-50" in my life, no equal share of giving and receiving. If I depended on people appreciating me, I would've stopped a long time ago.

And that is precisely the fond desire of so many good people. Good people like to help others. At the time they're actually responding to needs, their kindness is spontaneous and commendable. But then—afterward—they want to be praised for it. That's when they can poison the good instincts they began with. Because they worked hard to be helpful, they want people to make a big fuss over them. When it doesn't happen, they get depressed, as though they were cheated out of what was their due. Then they succumb to a mood of self-pity. Then they don't love so well, or care so much.

I'm not faulting them (and I'm not faulting you) for feeling bad when people treat you as a nobody after you were kind to them. You can't help feeling manipulated, as though you were a "thing," not a person. I also feel used when I'm treated that way.

So I don't fault the feeling, but rather the demand that goodness be rewarded. I'm faulting those who lay down conditions for their thoughtfulness, who say "As long as you appreciate me, I'll help you; but if you won't do so, I'll sulk...and I'll become depressed because you've treated me coldly after all I've done for you!"

The demand for rewards is Phariseeism, even when it comes after the good deed has been done. The parable I told focuses on the problem and the timing of the problem. The servant out in the fields was not troublesome while he was doing his chores, but when the work was finished he wanted his master (and the rest of the household) to put on the apron and serve him.

That's the big danger for good people such as yourself. You can get soured on life when others seem to be uncaring. This happens especially after you've been working hard and you're tired...and maybe your nerves are frayed.

At such times, remember my parable. Don't expect compensations for being kind. When you're appreciated, fine. When others notice what you've done, and thank you for it (or thank you in practical ways by assisting you), fine. I rejoice with you. But don't expect it.

Rewards come later, much later than you think. Keep going. Your faith will increase, as long as you guard yourself against discouragement . . . and keep your eyes fixed on the responsibilities—not the rewards—of love.

I pray for you now, and I'll always pray, that you'll continue to grow in my discipleship:

Lord God, my Father . . . look with love upon my disciples, my friends.

They always seem to start so well, and then they falter. They get so down when others don't make a fuss over them—when their hopes to be appreciated aren't satisfied.

Encourage them, so that they will not grow weary of doing good. Let their faith increase. Let their patience withstand the lack of human consolations.

Let them continue even better than they began: to love with never a thought for gain, to live without a complaint about bad treatment. Amen.

Love,
Jesus

LETTER 27

As Jesus continued on his journey to Jerusalem, ten lepers met him and cried out, "Jesus, Master, have pity on us." Jesus [did so; and on their way] they were made clean. . . . One of them, seeing that he was made clean, returned, fell on his face at the feet of Jesus, giving thanks. Jesus said, "Were not all ten made clean? Where are the other nine? Has no one been found to return and give thanks, except this (one)?"

Luke 17:11-19

*   *   *

Border of Samaria and Galilee
After supper
Novemeber 11

Dear Disciple, my Friend,

I'm not taking back anything I wrote you yesterday. The warning stands. The greatest temptation for good people still is—and always will be—the desire that God, and others, thank us "after all we've done for them." No matter how demanding the service we give, we must not look for rewards of any kind, not even the reward of being appreciated.

As you remember, I said something to the effect that "We can't help feeling bad when people snub us, after we spent time and effort doing good for them." I said it, and meant it. But something happened to me today that makes me want to state it even more strongly. Just like the other aspects of the passion I've mentioned in these letters, it's one thing to write about them, it's much more difficult to endure them.

The event was simple enough in itself; It was its significance that shook me. We continued toward Jerusalem, my disciples and I. Ten lepers came out of nowhere, pleading that I heal them. I did. I did it in the right way, too. Not wanting to take over legitimate authority, I told them to present themselves to the priests, so that they could be given "medical clearance" and be able to return to ordinary life.

On their way, they were cleansed of their contagious sores. I think they all were very happy about it...but I only know about one, the one who came back to tell me he was grateful.

No doubt, the other nine will thank me in their own way. I visualize them celebrating with their friends and family. I can see them, a couple of years from now, raising a glass of wine and calling out my name in some tavern, telling the story of their good fortune.

"In their own way!" So many people after them will do the same. They won't bother to worship the Father as I've instructed them. Too much trouble. They'll do it only as it pleases them.

One out of ten returned to thank me in a way that I could see and feel and rejoice in. One out of ten! That's hard to take. Of course, I must practice what I preach, and I did. I cured the lepers because I loved them...not because I wanted any reward from them.

Just the same, it hurts. When only one came back, I felt a hollowness in my heart. It wasn't a sting or a barb; it was like the stomach aware of its emptiness when it is hungry. I was tempted to say, "Why am I doing all this? Who cares, anyway? I push myself, dawn to dusk, to help people, to encourage them, to heal them from their sicknesses. As soon as they get what they want, I am forgotten as though I didn't even exist."

For a few moments, I was tempted with these thoughts. . . .
You've been tempted the same way, and you'll be tempted in the future, also. Each time is happens, you'll feel like giving up on everybody. Ingratitude knocks the wind right out of your sails. It causes a listlessness in the energy system. It's part of your passion. . .my passion, too.

Never mind. Keep going. Keep loving. Even if only a few show appreciation for you—even if only one person in the whole world of your lifetime shows it—consider it enough. We must love, you and I, whether anybody loves us in return or not.

When I'm lifted up to heaven, this is the prayer I'll pray for you and for all who'll suffer like you:

Lord God, my Father. . .look with love upon my disciples, my friends.
Fill up the hollowness of their hearts with the nourishment of my Spirit.

They feel as I felt after I cured ten lepers and only one said thanks. They wonder, right now, about themselves. They doubt their value. Their feeling is that if nobody seems to care about them, why should they care any more.

The feeling will pass; but help them so that it will pass more quickly. Let them be assured of my gratitude for them, even more strongly than they are sure of their present disappointment.

Remind them that I am with them always—helping them to suffer through the humiliation of ingratitude. Amen.

Love,
Jesus

LETTER 28

[As he continued toward Jerusalem] Jesus told his disciples a parable, to the effect that they ought always to pray, and not lose heart: "In a certain city was a judge...and a widow kept coming to him....For a while, he refused her; but afterward, he said to himself, 'Though I neither fear God nor regard man...I will grant the plea of this widow, or else she will wear me out!' And will God not vindicate [those] who cry to him, day and night? Will he delay long over them? I tell you, he will speedily [hear their prayers]. Nevertheless, when the Son of Man comes, will he find faith on earth?"

Luke 18:1-8

*   *   *

A deserted barn
Somewhere in Samaria
Late
November 21

Dear Disciple, my Friend,

I wish my mother were here tonight. This was a day we always celebrated together, the anniversary of her first day of school. She was a young girl when she went to Jerusalem to be taught by the Pharisees and their scribes.

They did a marvelous job. (As you know, not all of them were bad.) Mary was always grateful for her education. Every November 21, she'd tell me how she learned to pray and how she grew in wisdom and grace before God and people.

I need to remember her story. Today was very hard. I can see very clearly now how difficult it is not to lose heart. My disciples and I were alone all day. I told them the parable I was saving for just the right time. Today was it. I thought it would convince them my Father's trustworthiness. If even the worst specimen of humanity—a wicked judge—will do the right thing if someone pesters him enough... what will my kind Father do for those who ask him for favors?

I thought I needed only to remind them how much better my Father is than anyone else. But my story didn't help them much. I could see it in their faces. Their tendency to get discouraged was much stronger than all my words of assurance.

That's when I blurted out the last statement. It was a shocker...even to me. It was't on the tip of my tongue; it came from deep within my heart. "When I present myself to the people, will I find any faith on earth? (...Will there be anyone who'll take hold of my strength and let me be the source of their life? Anyone at all?")

The apostles were embarrassed by my sudden outburst. They know how dismayed I am by the waning of enthusiasm, but they can't seem to understand me any more. They don't comprehend the extent of the passion I'm suffering as I continue to Jerusalem.

I'm so glad I remember my mother. Hers is the faith I have found on earth. She's still with me and she'll be with the disciples when I am lifted up. Her conviction will strengthen theirs. So my work is worth the effort. I must be patient...always patient.

It's good to think of a loved one—family or friend—when situations look as bleak as they do are right now. You'll have moments when you'll embarrass people by your sadness, which was caused by a lot of things crowding in on you. They can't understand—they won't even discuss—the battle between trust and despair going on inside you.

You'll wonder, "What am I doing it all for? Who's with me?" When others lose heart in you, it's tempting to lose heart in yourself. That's the time to recall those connections-in-love you have in your memory. That can keep you going.

I remember my mother. You remember her, too...and remember all the good people in your life. You know them. Let them "come alive" in your thoughts. They'll help....

And don't forget me. Be aware of my inspirations. I'm present to you and to my Father—both. In this double-presence, I pray for you:

Lord God, my Father...look with love upon my disciples, my friends.

They have so many dismal looks thrown at them; they need our look of love.

Friends and their own family sometimes give up on them, get down on them, or somehow fail to help them.

You help them, Father. Urge them to grow in the good they have even though others don't think they're all that good.

Let them experience our kindliness toward them. And my mother's kindness, too. And all the many reasons they have never to stop praying—never to lose heart. Amen.

Love,
Jesus

LETTER 29

[As he continued on his journey] Jesus told this parable to some who trusted in themselves...and despised others: "Two men went up into the temple to pray....The Pharisee prayed thus with himself: God, I thank you that I am not like other men: extortioners, dishonest, adulterers, or like this tax collector....But the tax collector, standing far off...beat his breast, saying: 'God, be merciful to me, a sinner.' I tell you...everyone who exalts himself shall be humbled, but he who humbles himself shall be exalted.

Luke 18:9-14

*   *   *

A friend's house
Northeast Judea
Late afternoon
November 30

Dear Disciple, my Friend,

The apostles are somewhat relieved today. I seem to be my old self again, preaching to the people, rebuking the Pharisees (instead of them). "All is well," they think. "No more emphasis on the passion." Not so. They just don't understand me yet.

Oh, I can appreciate that I seem to have changed. They figured I was just moping around for a week, disgusted with life and with them and everything. I wasn't moping. The realization that "even after all my works of love, I will not find much faith on earth" did hit me hard. I didn't want to talk much for a while. I distanced myself, made a private retreat, prayed in silence. I let them handle the preaching and healing.

Now I'm back again. I must continue. But I'm still talking about the passion. This is the first time I've taught in ten days. My message is the same. I just spelled out why I don't find much faith.

You know how it feels to be ignored when those you want to talk to can't seem to find any place in their hearts to hear you. They use up all available energy complaining, especially about other people. They go to work and find fault with their boss; they go down the street to see what's wrong with the neighbors; they nag their family, using the same tactic I mentioned in the parable. Instead of saying "I'm so glad I'm better than that tax collector," they turn it around. The nag asks, "Why aren't you as good as, as smart as, or as thoughtful as I am?"

Newspapers give them reason to find fault with the world. Religious worship (whether they're present at it or not) gives them cause to find fault with those in church. Everything is grist for the mill.

Of course, it's pride. Just like the braggart in my parable, every fault-finder is irreparably convinced of her self-righteousness. How else can the agitator criticize others with such certainty. . .unless she feels superior to her targets?

Pride may be the source of the trouble, but the outcome is usually inertia. All energy is used up diagnosing other people's imperfections. Then you come on the scene, all ready to tell them something important, and they can't hear you. In fact, you—as you—don't even exist. You're just a function; your only role is to provide an audience so they can tell you how awful other people are.

You know how it feels to be used in this way. I know it, too. Through all generations, so many hearts will be blocked off from me because of envy, gossip, criticism, complaints about wrong done, and bickering about someone else's evil ways.

There's not much I can do about it; I just tell another parable and pray it takes hold. I do hope people will stop making comparisons between themselves and others. (They usually compare themselves at their best, and note the behavior of other people at their worst!)

I can't do much to change their hearts; I can only try to persuade them not to waste so much energy on others, and to start attending to their own improvement. Ultimately, I'll die for them so that

74

they'll realize I've given my life for the forgiveness of their sins.

When I return to my Father, I'll pray you don't block me off with some kind of self-righteousness. And I'll pray you won't have to suffer too much when others block you off the same way:

Lord God, my Father...look with love upon my disciples, my friends.

They get tired, sometimes, from all the blah, blah, blah ringing in their ears. They want to shout out to the cantankerous: "Please stop using me as your crabbing-post. And get off the hobby horses of your gripes. And talk to me...and let us grow together." But they don't say such things. They only suffer.

Father, don't let them join the list of fault-finders. Give them a calm to live in. Show them a space of silence...so that they may hear my gospel, and know my love, and be able to thank you for your mercy. Amen.

Love,
Jesus

LETTER 30

Jesus entered Jericho and was passing through [on his way to Jerusalem]. And there was a man, Zacchaeus; he was a chief tax-collector and rich. He climbed a sycamore tree....Jesus looked up and said to him. "Zacchaeus, hurry and come down, for I must stay in your house today." ...He recieved him joyfully. And when [the Pharisees saw it] they all murmured: "He has gone to be the guest of a man who is a sinner!"

Luke 19:1-10

*   *   *

Zacchaeus's house
Jericho
Dusk
December 15

Dear Disciple, my Friend,

It's been a lovely day for me. Instead of being wet and windy, it was sunny and warm. December seemed like April. Instead of a hurried meal over the open fire, I had one of the best roast lamb dinners ever. And instead of facing the downcast looks of my apostles, the puzzled frowns of the people, and the hostile stares of my enemies, I closed the doors on all of that and enjoyed a good long afternoon with one of the wittiest, wisest, and holiest men I've met.

Zacchaeus is his name. I wish you could meet him. Oh yes, the "upright people" call him shrewd and wicked, and he was that. His wit was sometimes used for selfish purposes. I've yet to know a person who wasn't a sinner—you're one yourself—but I forgave him his sins. He's paying back fourfold anyone he's cheated.

Once that was settled, he relaxed. Then his good side streamed out of him. He's a charming storyteller, and had many good ideas about how I can get the jump on those who try to trip me up. (He's a pro at it.)

He's resourceful, too. I could see that when I spotted him perched in that sycamore tree. Right then I decided that he was a man after my own heart. Nothing—not even the fact that he made a fool of himself—nothing would prevent him from reaching me. I wanted to know more about him, so I invited myself to his home.

I never did this before. I like to eat out, but except for today I always waited to be asked. Today was different; I needed a break in the routine. I also wanted his companionship. If he could risk ridicule to see me. I could do the same for him.

And ridicule is what I'll get. This is the passion I want to tell you about. The Pharisees have already started murmuring. They have another pin to stick in me. I've become a friend of the class of people they can't stand. How can I be any good if I associate with those whom "good people" claim are no good? This is the reasoning of bigots.

I'm continually cut off by narrow-mindedness. So many people assume that God (and his Messiah) must love whatever they love . . . and despise the same people they despise. If these self-righteous individuals ever realize how many "disgusting people" (as they call them) will be in heaven, they'll probably refuse to live there!

You've also been the butt of ridicule because you became a friend of someone the influential people don't like. This suffering exists from childhood to old age. Just reach out and shake hands with a member of the "out group," or walk home with them, or have lunch with them and you'll get nasty treatment from the "in group."

Know-it-alls distress me just as they distress you. Because I enjoyed myself this afternoon, the Pharisees will fault me. That's to be expected. Whether the man I dined with was acceptable or not, I should've been someplace else, in their opinion. They'll snipe at anything.

My apostles, too, will look at me with long faces. Oh, they won't say anything, but their gestures will scold me: "Where were you! You left us stuck with all this work and all these people...and you were out enjoying yourself. We never get the day off. It's not fair!"

You know what I mean. You've experienced such things. The very people who urge you to "relax once in a while" are the ones who'll complain if you do just that. They tell you to learn how to say no to people once in a while...but they never want you to say no to them. You should've stayed up, they'll tell you. You should've been right there by the telephone when they wanted you. Things like that. Almost every time you take the day off just for yourself, there'll be some people (even friends and family) who'll second-guess you.

This hurts, but it's no big deal. The psychological passion is made up of little hurts, not only big ones.

Never mind. Keep going. There'll always be people who are, as they put it, "disappointed in you." I understand how it feels to be picked on because such things. I'll be with you in my Spirit and in my prayer to God:

Lord God, my Father...look with love upon my disciples, my friends.

So often there's some kind of shadow cast on their simple joys. If they take a break from the routine—even a half-day off—they will have 'know betters' who want to tell them what they should have done instead. And if they make a friend of someone they don't like, the jealous ones will consider them unfaithful, and bigots will resort to gossip.

Father, don't let them get upset by this. If the time off or the friendship found has proved to be restorative and good, then it was good. They are blessed for it.

Let them be at peace...remembering that peace on earth can never come without some passion. World without suffering, joys without shadows, can only come at the end of the journey— theirs and mine. Amen.

Love,
Jesus

LETTER 31

[As the disciples were listening] Jesus proceeded to tell them a parable because he was near to Jerusalem, and because they supposed that the kingdom of God was to appear immediately. [The parables of a)Ten servants given money to trade with "until the master returned," b)Certain citizens who did not want the nobleman to rule over them.]

And when he had said this parable, he went on ahead, going up to Jerusalem....And when he drew near and saw the city, he wept over it, saying: "Would that even today you knew the things that make for your peace. But now they are hidden from your eyes...because you did not know the time of your visitation."

Luke 19:11,28, 41-44

*   *   *

Outskirts of Jerusalem
Late
February 2
(The anniversary of my presentation
in the Temple)

Dear Disciple, my Friend,

This is it. I've finally made it to the city where I'll be lifted up. It's not the end, exactly; that'll wait until the Passover. It's time to complete the education of my apostles, to explain the meaning of my parables by the parable I spoke to them today...time to do many things.

I feel like saying "This is it" in terms of my psychological passion, too. In a capsulated form, all I've suffered during my journey has been expressed on this one day. I was rejected three different ways by three different groups of people.

One group was the ordinary citizens. They're the reason I wept. No matter how many disabled people I cured, no matter how well I taught, I couldn't reach most of those I've come here to love. They didn't respond to my visitation.

Another group was the notables of the land. Their rebuke of me is the story of the second parable I told today. They're the "deputation" that doesn't want me to rule them. There are about 600 influential people living in Jerusalem and surroundings. I've favorably impressed only two of them: Joseph of Arimethea and Nicodemus.

That's not a good record. Think about it, my disciple, my friend, the next time you're discouraged because you aren't impressing those you want to impress...or because you can't help or teach the people you'd like to. Remember, the disciple can't be greater than the master. I reached only two out of 600! So it wouldn't be wise for you to expect a perfect record. And it would be a disaster if you got depressed, because you can't win them all.

I don't blame you for being sad. (After all, I wept.) But I will blame you if you stop just because you're rejected. It isn't stopping me; it can't stop you.

The third group to be mentioned in this summary is the most important group of all, my disciples. The main reason I told them the parable (indeed, the main reason I've told most of my parables) is to warn them against impatience.

My Father does his work of grace through me, but it takes time. Free will's at stake. Love never forces anyone, and so the results of love never happen as easily or as quickly as one would wish.

Waiting *is* the passion. The apostles "want the kingdom of God to appear immediately." They want "instant happiness"...everything fixed just nicely...people being thoughtful of each other...life without worries, love without pain. It doesn't happen that way; so they get irritated. My word is "Wait!"; their word is "Now!" One of these words has to go.

You know how it feels when you're struggling with a complex situation that demands a cautious sensitivity. You have to balance certain opposing inclinations; you have to wait for certain answers. It's a delicate operation. And what a struggle within you when friends and family—not realizing the nature of your work—call for immediate results. They want you to be an instant winner.

It hurts to be so misunderstood. I know. I'm writing you so that when it happens to you, you won't be crushed by it. The successful outcome of any project takes time, especially if free will is involved. Take the time. Be thorough in your preparations, even though certain individuals try to get you to cut corners because they want no delays. Their demands are part of your passion.

But please, my friend, don't be part of my passion any more. Be patient with me. The reason your life isn't completely happy is because of certain things I can't control: the presence of evil in the world (free will again!), and the fact that few people are willing to comply with the prime condition for prayers to be answered: that we must forgive all those who've harmed us.

I'm working to establish peace and love. I offer pardon to all who ask for it (as long as they agree to pardon others). This doesn't happen overnight. It's difficult to be patient. It's very difficult to forgive those who've harmed you.

When you think of me, be kind. Consider how I labored to put stamina into the hearts of my first disciples...how I pleaded with them to persevere, despite delays.

And consider yourself instructed by the same parables, by the same urgency on my part. Let's make a bargain: You promise not to pressure me with your impatience, and I'll make sure that you have my strength when you're pressured by the kind of pushiness I've had to put up with.

You'll have my strength. You'll have my prayer:

Lord God, my Father...look with love upon my disciples, my friends.

They hurt from two kinds of hurriedness. They want me to hurry things up for them, so that their world will be less troublesome. And they are hurting because friends are trying to rush them, pushing them into panic when the need is for peace.

Give them our peace, Father. Don't deliver them over to the fast pace of their world. Love, like life itself, is a subtle thing; it takes time.

Give them the time...and the patience to use time well.
Amen.

Love,
Jesus

LETTER 32

Jesus said: "Heaven and earth will pass away, but my words will
not pass away. So take heed to yourselves, lest your hearts be
overburdened with self-indulgence and drunkenness and the
cares of this life...Watch, praying at all times, that you may be
accounted worthy...." Now in the daytime he was teaching in
the temple; but he would...spend the nights on the mountain
called Olivet. And all the people came to him early in the morning, in the temple, to hear him.

Luke 21: 34-38

*   *   *

Mount Olivet
Late
Mid-March

Dear Disciple, my Friend,

The Mount of Olives is my headquarters from now on. I won't
be here much longer. My journey's ended...except for a few more
days of commuting to Jerusalem to do a job that means only drudgery
and dread for me.

This is what I want to tell you about. It means taking myself
away from one more hour of much needed rest, but you're worth it.
And the matter I want to write you about is worth it also.

I must be in Jerusalem by dawn! Before dawn, I'll get up, pray,
gather all my wits about me, and meet a throng of people in the temple
area.

For hours on end, I'll endure an experience that you'd under-stand as a "Congressional Inquest." Suppose the President of the United States wants someone to be Secretary of State. But the people don't want him, and the political leaders definitely don't want him. Imagine the ordeal as Congress bears down on him, trying to make him look unworthy or unfit.

My ordeal is similar. I mention it just so you'd get a sense of what's going on . . . and so, imagine how I dread getting ready for the next day.

I'm not implying that your ordinary situations will ever get as bad as these last days of mine. But there are times when you've felt the intensity of what I'm experiencing. You've experienced it yourself. Sometimes, you don't even want to put your shoes on. You groan just getting up. Another day! Another carbon copy of the same old grind. No relief. You go to work and get no satisfaction. You face the same suspicions on the part of your superiors, the same lack of cooperation on the part of fellow workers, the same frustration from a job not very well done.

I know. These last days commuting to Jerusalem—I'm going through it too. My "supervisors" are putting me through their inquest. The ordinary people (my disciples, too) are so overburdened by self-indulgence and anxieties that they're no match for the single-minded hatred of the Pharisees. My revelation of God as the Father of mercy is falling on stony ground.

I write this to tell you we're in it together whenever such a dreadful passion comes up in your life . . . when "too much work" com-bines with "no satisfaction and no cooperation." Don't give up because you're so discouraged. Keep going. Those days when you don't even feel like getting out of bed, force yourself to get going.

I'm not saying that the psychological passion will pass; it isn't passing for me. I'm saying that courage is the only answer. I'll give you mine. You'll receive my determination to do good, although you'll get no consolation from it, none at all.

Trust me. You'll benefit, even in your sadness, from the prayer I'll pray for you in heaven:

Lord God, my Father . . . look with love upon my disciples, my friends.

Give them the staying power you gave me, during my last few days on earth.

They suffer very much sometimes. Oh, not from the boredom of routine. They can handle those everyday demands. But sometimes it seems like the drudgery is too much. Their work means nothing to them. Friends are so self-indulgent that they don't care. From dawn to dark, they plod ahead without support, without job-satisfaction.

You be their support, my Father, when all else fails them. You be the reason for their valued constancy.

Give them if—in their faith—foreknowledge of the outcome, here...after the hardships they've had to undergo. Amen.

Love,
Jesus

LETTER 33

When the hour had come, Jesus reclined at table with his twelve apostles. And he said to them: "I have earnestly desired to eat this passover with you before I suffer...But behold, the hand of him who betrays me is with me...Woe to that man by whom I will be betrayed...." Now there arose a dispute among the apostles, as to which of them was reputed to be the greatest....

Luke 22:21-24

*   *   *

Mount Olivet
Wednesday, late
The evening before
my Last Supper

Dear Disciple, my Friend,

The journey's over. I suppose I should've stopped writing two or three letters back. I'm no longer on the move. The "psychological passion" I've been suffering will soon give way to the more brutal kind: my passion to the death.

It's not martyrdom my Father asks of you. But there are some related sufferings you'll endure that are very much like the kind of hurts mentioned in these letters. I want to point them out to you. You might miss them; they could be overshadowed by the larger events of these last days.

From now on, my letters will be written before the things actually take place. I won't have the time or opportunity to write afterward. I know what's coming up, well enough to make a good guess at it. I must steel myself. Writing to you helps.

The time for my betrayal is at hand. You know how it feels to be betrayed, but I am not writing about this. I've already touched on it in some of my other letters. Besides, it is too painful to mention my feelings, now; it is too personal. I can only say that it, too, is part of my passion. I must continue. So must you.

However, there is something else, a sideline of tomorrow, that I want to mention. It is all the other things that accompany betrayal. If it were only Judas who did me in, I think I could manage more easily. After all, one out of twelve is a good average. But the other eleven will depress me also.

As soon as I mention betrayal, all my apostles will collapse. I am saving my most important words for the most important night of my life, our Last Supper together. My disciples won't even be listening. They'll start disputing with one another, quarreling among themselves like a bunch of unruly children! They won't be thinking about me or gathering around to support me. No, they'll be thinking mostly about their own crushed hopes...and the severed ranks that one traitor has caused...and their own positions of prominence, now that there's an opening for a new Secretary of the Treasury in my "cabinet."

It's the breakdown of all my disciples that causes me such added pain. You know how it is. When you feel something very deeply— maybe a betrayal, maybe the prospect of a lingering illness (or death itself), maybe the severe challenge of pulling up roots and starting a brand new life, whatever it may be—there are times when you need the support of friends as never before.

And they are not with you. They think of your crisis only as it involves themselves. They spend all their energy thinking of how they can survive, instead of how they can assist you.

This hurts. There's nothing you can do about it. You must accept your friends as they are, with all their weaknesses. This is the passion, too.

I wanted to write you this, beforehand. By doing so, I hope you will understand even better how much I love you . . . and that you'll accept me as your source of courage when you endure sufferings like mine.

I will always be with you. Don't worry. I will send you my Holy Spirit, my Wisdom and my Courage. We will help you understand what true love is; we'll help you prove your love under trials patiently endured:

Lord God, my Father . . . look with love upon my disciples, my friends.

Don't let them surrender their will to live when they are betrayed, or when life itself seems to betray them. Help them continue, despite their anguish.

And don't let them drown in the "second wave" of their much-saddening experience—when friends they had counted on are too busy with their own panic about survival to have much time for them. Help them survive, as you helped me. Let them understand that they must maintain love, even when life itself is periled.

Our Spirit will be with them. We'll see to it. And when they die, our same Spirit will raise them up, like me, beyond all chance of any more betrayals, and free from the discomfitures of their (sometimes) comforting-less friends. Amen.

Love,

Jesus

LETTER 34

Jesus said [to his eleven apostles]: "You have continued with me in my trials. And I appoint you a kingdom . . . so that you may eat and drink at my table. . . . And the Lord said [to Peter]: "Simon, Simon, behold Satan has desired to have you, that he may sift you as wheat. But I have prayed for you, that your faith may not fail...and when you have turned [back to me] again, you my strengthen your brethren."

Luke 22:28-32

*   *   *

Mount Olivet
Wednesday, later
The evening before
my Last Supper

Dear Disciple, my Friend,

Here is another letter tonight. I can't sleep anyway. I'll be very busy tomorrow. I want to get this off to you right now.

The main reason for putting these thoughts on paper is to encourage you, but I also do it to encourage myself. The very fact that I'm expressing myself like this helps my strength.

I suggest you do the same. Write letters to me as I'm writing to you. It's a good form of prayer; it helps to develop trust in God, and it helps wisdom to emerge. The shaping of words on paper stimulates energy. It also (as in my case tonight) builds up a better resolve to be at the service of friends.

I must encourage my apostles tomorrow. Unless I give them some sense of their value—some anchor for their hope—they will falter beyond recovery. I must not become too saddened because they can't seem to encourage me. I wish they could, but their hearts are too heavy. I must encourage them.

I will remind them that they have a special place in my kingdom. They've continued with me through all my trials, all the psychological suffering of my journey to Jerusalem. They weren't perfect, but they remained loyal, despite their murmurings and misgivings. So the Father loves them; he will never leave them orphans. They will sit at my table in the eternal kingdom.

And I'll have special words of encouragement for Simon Peter. He'll need it most, because he's the leader...and because he'll be the most devastated. I will tell him about my prayer for him tonight. I know he will disappoint me Friday, but I also know that his basic goodness and fine leadership qualities will eventually show themselves.

In time, he will prove to be a man after my own heart.

Tomorrow, I will remind him—all eleven of them—that I never regretted selecting them. I am proud of them, even with their occasional outbursts of temper and their quarrels and doubts.

I will do this tomorrow, even though it will be tempting to tell them off.

You must never think I've been blissfully freed from such psychological pressures. I feel things just as you do. I don't like it any more than you do...when you are drained from overwork and have been supporting other people for a long time...and you'd like to have others give you some support once in a while...but they can't because they're relying on you...so you have to let go of your claims on them and answer to their needs. Such self-denial on your part takes high resolve. You must become a person of deep prayer in order to keep going, and keep on giving, in spite of the drain on your energy.

I will do it. Even when they fall asleep on me, I will do it, and do it well. My apostles will be given hope to hang on to. I promise to pray for Simon Peter. I will keep my promise, and he will be strengthened.

So will you. My pledge of prayer is my testament to you, as well. When I go to my Father, I will ask that your faith may never fail. And once you have been tested and proven true, I want you to strengthen others...as Simon Peter will do next Pentecost...as I will do Friday, two days from now:

Lord God, my Father...look with love upon my disciples, my friends.

It's hard, sometimes, for them to face the day ahead. They have been serving others for so long, encouraging them with words and deeds. Like a pelican feeding its young with its own heart, they have been nourishing others with all the resourcefulness they have. They get tired for all this. Sometimes they give encouragement, but they seldom get it.

We are the only ones left, Father. You and I. Send them our Spirit. Give them an "inside way" to know about love. Let them locate the deeper strength they didn't know was in them.

Then they will be able to do for others...because of what I, first, have done for them. Amen.

Love,
Jesus

LETTER 35

Jesus, according to his custom, went to the Mount of Olives....He withdrew from his disciples, and kneeling down, he began to pray: "Father, if you are willing, remove this cup from me; yet not my will, but yours, be done." ...And his sweat became as drops of blood running down upon the ground.

Luke 22:39-44

*   *   *

Mount Olivet
Wednesday, later still
The evening before
my Last Supper

Dear Disciple, my Friend,

Interesting. In a way, I'm exhilarated by the prospect of my ordeal tomorrow in this same Garden of Olives. I know it will be extremely painful, but I have a sense of victory.

My last temptation will be a carbon copy of all the others. Satan will be up to the same old tricks. He started me off with discouragement on a grand scale. That was almost three years ago, after my forty days in the desert. He showed me all the kingdoms of the world that I would lose unless I followed his policy. He urged me to dazzle people with a flashy miracle, hurling myself off the parapet of the temple to get quick results. He told me to turn stones into bread, reasoning that once I knew I could do such a trick, I'd be successful in a guerilla war because my soldiers could depend on daily rations.

Oh, he was clever! Each of these temptations pointed out the contrast between winning and losing. If I chose to love people, I would lose; if I decided to control them, I would win.

On the surface, the majority of the world is impressed by promises and power. It considers love a weakness. If I assured people that they'd be given bread, I could be acclaimed their Christ. If I manipulated them with political clout and threats of punishment (the way all other kingdoms are ruled) I could be acclaimed king. If I jumped from the roof of the temple and let angels keep me safe, I could be the rallying point of their religious fervor, because allegiance to a miracle worker would make them feel important.

But if I go the way of love—without clout, without promise of security in this world, without the mesmerizing effect of flashy miracles—I will be a loser.

That was my original temptation, the prototype of all the others. Satan wanted me to change my resolve and tactics. Force, he insisted, was the only way to win people over. The alternative would be deaf ears, dull hearts...and, for myself, the feeling of being stranded...and death on a cross.

It was only the first of my temptations. I won only the initial skirmish against the devil of discouragement. (Satan left me, as you know, for other "more favorable opportunities.")

But the interesting thing is that all the other temptations were really the same. Oh, there were different events that triggered disappointment over my lack of results. (That's why I've written you so many letters.) Specific situations, and the stress that each puts on the soul, were different. But the basic urgency to give up—because true love seems to be a "loser"—was the same.

"See?" I could hear Satan saying to me, "See where love gets you? You still can do so little for so few...people still want to praise you for the wrong reasons...they still refuse to listen...the whole world of the future is summed up by the response of those nine out of ten lepers who didn't bother to return to you....Even if you died and then rose from death, the world will still be like those five brothers of the rich man: They won't pay one bit of attention!"

Yes, my disciple, my friend, that is the suffering I have wrestled with for three long years, especially since I began my last journey to Jerusalem. I know I will be mocked and scourged and men will spit at me. It will be painful. But the worst pain is the same as all the others: that I have so little to show for all I've tried to do.

You know the hurt of it. You have experienced the like of it. It's so hard to be battling the same old thing—over and over and over.

I have good news and bad news about your recurrent grief. The bad news is that you will never be freed of it. The devil will do to you what he did to me; he'll keep coming back for what he thinks is "a more favorable opportunity."

The good news is that temptations will diminish in their power to control you. Oh, the suffering can become even more intense. (I have experienced nothing like what will happen to me in the next two days.) But the power to shake you will grow weaker...because you will be stronger each time you refuse to quit on life.

Be encouraged by this. You might be made more lonely, more frustrated, more filled with illness and incapacities, but temptations will little by little be easier to handle. As surely as I sense the victory of Easter in my Garden of Gethsemane, I'll help you to sense the same.

I wanted to write you ahead of time, so that you would not miss the significance of my agony...or the taste of my triumph.

Keep going, no matter what the odds. Love, when it is real love, does a lot of losing...but it is never a loser. People who misuse power end up being the losers, for death (as well as old age, or even the whims of chance) puts an end to power. But love does not depend on tangible results, not really. It suffers from the lack of results, but it doesn't need results to know its value.

Besides, I know I'm not a complete failure. My mother will enjoy eternal life because of what I do. If there were nobody else, she would be worth it. You will be made a child of God also—and countless others with you.

I must do what I must do. I could not live with myself (and my Father would not find me acceptable) unless I loved without conditions.

It is the same with you: the same demands for love, the same Spirit to see it through, the same promise of God's approval, the same victory over all distress, even over death itself.

I will see to it. I am in your corner, and in your heart, each time you wrestle with the devil of discouragement. You will be sustained as I will be sustained...tomorrow:

Lord God, my Father...look with love upon my disciples, my friends.

Things pile up sometimes. They get downhearted because of the relentlessness of the same old thing, the same old temptation never letting up:

They thought they solved their money problems, but another crisis comes, and they are still broke!

They thought they conquered their impatience, and there they go again!

They thought they forgave the person who hurt them, but then the wound with its hateful memories comes back to haunt them one more time!

They thought they found life worth living; then something else occurs to make them doubt it!

Don't let them get downed by these "Gethsemanes." Don't let them buckle under. Let my friends strain forward to live even more purely, to share their love even more obviously.

You gave me the power to do just this. Give them the power to do the same. Love is worth it. You are worth it, Father. And they—with victory over death in sight—they are worth it to themselves. Amen.

Love,
Jesus

LETTER 36

They led Jesus away to be crucified. Now a great crowd of people was following him... [among them] women who were wailing and lamenting him. But Jesus, turning to them, said: Daughters of Jerusalem, do not weep for me, but for yourselves and for your children...."

Luke 23:27-31

*   *   *

Mount Olivet
Thursday, mid-afternoon
The day of my Last Supper

Dear Disciple, my Friend,

The world is full of anticlimaxes. I thought I'd said it all last night, all there was to say. I summed it up well for you and for myself. I had prepared myself for the ultimate test of Satan. I was ready...so I thought.

Then, this morning, something unforeseen happened. It quite unnerved me. It was really nothing in itself. (These things usually are, objectively speaking, nothing in themselves.) But it prodded all the other sorrows mentioned in my last letter, and gave them a further jolt. It was the "straw" that almost broke my back.

I was walking through the streets of Jerusalem on my last trip to the temple precincts. I overheard a group of women planning their work of mercy for tomorrow. They're good women and my Father will bless them for their thoughtfulness. They knew I'm going to be crucified, and they felt sorry for me. They do this for all victims condemned to die; it's their work of mercy. They'll position themselves at the most strategic corner on my way to Calvary. They'll weep for me...offer me some wine if the soldiers let them...show me how sad they are that I am brutalized.

They mean well, but their futile attempt to console me will only make me feel more miserable. It already has.

The contrast is what gets me. The women are, in a sense, a case of too little and too late. Just a handful of pious women doing their good deed for the day. As I heard them planning their strategy, many heavy thoughts were stirred. I began to wonder: "Where are the other people—the multitudes I fed in the desert, the many I cured? If there were only a fraction of those I've helped in the last three years...if only a fraction of them were around to make a protest march on my behalf...that would make the authorities change their tune. I taught them all, worked for them all. Where are they?

"And why aren't the leaders of my people as impressed with my innocence as these women are? After all, I've spent three long years establishing my credentials as the Christ. I'm the promised one the Pharisees and the scribes have prayed for, studied about, kept this nation pure of false worship so that Israel could greet me when I came.

"Then I did come, and they did not welcome me. I couldn't influence the influential people of my country. The compassion of these few women—strangers to me—only serves to mock my failure in reaching those I wanted so much to impress."

I have to tell you this (I hope you won't be shocked): For a brief moment this morning I felt like storming into their proceedings and telling them not to meet me. They'll only force me to reply to them, using up whatever strength I may have left.

I felt like yelling: "Don't bother! You're but one drop of water falling on the desert of my doom! Your feeble attempt to cheer me up only makes me more miserable, for it makes me think of my ratio of success; a few who care compared with thousands who don't.

"Don't ask me to respond to you!" I wanted to shout at them.

"You're only making things worse!"

Of course, I never said such things. They didn't even know I eavesdropped on them. But for a moment I wanted to say such things. I was tempted to . . . .

This is my last chance to write you before I celebrate the Passover. We're waiting for Peter and John to return. This is the last spare moment I'll have. It's a rather strange way to conclude; a bit anticlimactic. I suppose I should be more solemn, but suffering is seldom solemn. It is mostly sad, and usually surprising.

You know what I mean. In the strangest ways, the full burden of sorrow will throw its full weight on you, perhaps as it happened to me. Well-meaning people may try to cheer you up, but they don't do it right—they don't know how, or don't say the right things, or aren't the right people you want to say such things, or their feeble attempts to console you only point out how inconsolable you are.

Never mind. It was to hurt, for it measures your inability to escape from grief. But it can't stop you. Make sure you don't let your anger loose on them. Don't vent your frustration on those people who're trying to help you. Even if they aren't "the right ones," they deserve your love . . . and your civil response. My Father has strange ways of telling us that the so-called nobodies in our life are more important in his eyes than those we think are more important.

We must leave everything in my Father's hands. With whatever energy is left, we must continue to manifest our love in whatever ways we still can.

I must go now. Peter and John are coming back. Everything from now on will either be action or prayer to my Father, prayer that I can not interrupt.

Farewell. God will be with you. I promise you my love—always— and especially during those times when a surprising turn of events makes your sadness almost overwhelming:

Lord God, my Father . . . look with love upon my disciples, my friends.

I must now begin my sacrifice of love. Henceforth, I ask you, Father, to be my prayer for me. You know my heart. You know my concern for my disciples. Let all my prayers—written and unwritten—give nourishment to them in times of need.

I do not ask you to take them out of the world, not until they finish their work of love. I do not ask you to free them from suffering. You know best about such things. But I do ask you to deliver them from too much, and too soon, and too surprising.

And free them, finally, for the day that I, too, look forward to: for fullest life with you, and joy in its abundance. Amen.

Love,
Jesus

LETTER 37

It was now about the sixth hour, and there was darkness over the whole land until the ninth hour....And Jesus cried out with a loud voice and said, "Father, into your hands I commend my spirit." And having said this, he breathed his last.

Luke 23:44-46

*   *   *

Prison
Mid-morning
Good Friday

Dear Disciple, my Friend,

Surprise letter. I never thought I'd have the time or occasion to write you again. One of the soldiers who scourged me (in fact, he seemed more cruel than any of them) is an old friend of Judas.

He's guarding me, while I wait for Pilate to grant me an audience. He apologized for Judas. He also expressed regret for what all the soldiers did to me. "Only doing our duty," he said. Then he gave me writing material, as well as something to stop my bleeding. Thoughtful of him.

I've already written my mother. He'll make sure she gets it. Don't know how much time I have, so this may be hurried. Consider it a "postscript" to all my other letters.

(When I have sent you the Holy Spirit, you'll be able to understand what I'm going through these last days...and why I'm going through it.)

I just want to tell you that right now I'm glad I suffered all those psychological passions as I journeyed to Jerusalem. They were difficult at the time. On reflection, some of them seemed more painful than today. But they got me ready for today. They were a kind of "dress rehearsal," preparing me for my agony last night...and for the unfair allegations and the mockings of this morning...and for the crucifixion coming soon.

The way I continued through all the hardships in the past have steadied me in my resolve today. No one takes my life from me. I give it out of love. The devil hasn't broken my spirit, neither has the violence of my enemies, nor the insensitivity of those who turned their backs on me.

What I will say from my cross, I say to you right now: I commend my spirit to God my Father, trusting that he won't allow death to have its final word over me.

I sense the cohort of soldiers coming. Better finish. Just this: Know that your perseverance under trials—all those I've written about this year—will be "feathers in your cap" some day. You'll face death, too. At that ultimate moment, one of two things will happen. You'll give up in despair and rage against the meaninglessness of life, since all life ends with death. Either that...or you'll trust God's power to raise you up from death—to a fuller life, linked with mine.

If you go the way of trust, you can thank yourself (and me) that you continued to love even though you suffered from one or more of those daily hurts you had to put up with. They were your "dress rehearsals," preparing you for the greatest challenge of all—the one I must meet in a short time.

Farewell. I'll be with you in all distress. No time for a prayer, not now. I must seal this letter and leave it for my friend to take to Mary...and to you.

My prayer for you will be a silent one...from the cross. When I commend my spirit to the Father, I'm commending yours as well. Amen. Wait for my alleluia.

Love,

Jesus

LETTER 38

Very early on the first day of the week [some women] came to the tomb. . . . And looking up, they saw that the stone had been rolled back. . . . While they were perplexed about this, two men stood by them. . . and they said: "Why do you seek the living among the dead?"

Luke 24:1-6

*   *   *

My favorite hill in Galilee
Mid-afternoon
Easter

Dear Disciple, my Friend,

Happy Easter! It is for me. I want it to be for you. I'm waiting here in Galilee for my disciples to catch up to me. Had a lovely visit with my mother. She has gone home to get things ready for a big dinner. I've got some time on my hands and I thought I'd write you.

Strange, though, there isn't much I can say. I was dead. Now I'm alive. . .alive in a much livelier way than ever before. It's exhilarating! My body and feelings haven't gotten quite used to it yet.

I can't explain myself. (That's what makes this letter so hard to write.) For me to describe the nature of my life is as impossible as it would be for you to tell a six-year-old child about what you enjoy most as an adult.

Try to explain the quality of an adult love, a deep friendship, the capacity for wisdom and understanding that you've acquired through the years. Try to explain the complex reasons for your appreciation of a symphony or a work of art. The child would be puzzled and say, "What? No toys? No fights? No cookies? How could you have any fun?"

A child's imagination can visualize things only on the basis of personal experience. You'd end up shrugging your shoulders, saying, "Well, child, you'll have to grow up before you can understand." That's what I'm reduced to. You'll have to die first, and come up on the other side of life, as I did. Then—and only then—will you understand.

But I can tell you this much: Be ready for surprises. In fact, even on your side of life, be ready for surprises. Be very careful not to get stuck in the "tombs" of your misery. God and gloom don't mix. Wherever my Father and I are, moodiness must absent itself.

The angels told me about the shock Mary Magdalen and the other women had. They were expecting me to be in the tomb. They thought I was still dead...as dead as their hopes. They felt miserable, so they figured I was boxed in my misery as well.

They were surprised. I didn't fit the pattern of their expectations. Never have. Never will. The Easter message from my point of view is: "He is risen." The Easter message from your point of view is: "HE IS GONE."

Yes, gone. I'm not where you think. I'll never be contained by your dimensions. I'll always listen to your prayers. If you ask the Father anything in my name (and if you ask with faith and forgive all those who have done you harm), my Father will grant you what you ask. I'll always be with you.

But I won't always be with you in the ways you want me to be. Your wishes are too short-sighted sometimes. Too often, they're a product of laziness, or the desire to live without a worry in the world, or the demand that I deny my Father's gift of free will and force unpleasant people to suddenly be nice to you.

On the other hand, your ideas about me could be the same as the women a few hours ago. You can become so engulfed in your own woes, your enemies can treat you so unjustly, the calamaties of nature, wars, or the death of a dear one can so overwhelm you—in any of these cases, you may be tempted to think I'm as crushed as your own life seems to be.

But you'll find surprises waiting for you every time. I am not crushed. I'm not dead. I rose from death, and I'll raise you out of your dark nights and depressions, too—as long as you don't lose hope and let me surprise you by new turns of events.

You know by now (I've repeated it enough) that I can't change anybody's free will. When I was journeying to Jerusalem, I couldn't soften the heart of Judas, Pilate, or Herod. I couldn't snap my fingers and make the most unpleasant Pharisees turn into pleasant people. I couldn't even persuade my own disciples to stay awake with me during my night of agony. They fell asleep...and there was nothing I could do about it.

That's why I've written so many letters: to warn you that there are many things that even God can't do. He can't force anyone's free will and still be the God of his promise. People are to be loved, and, by love, be given every reason to be lovers in return. But never forced.

I'll be with you, so that you may know my victory over death and every kind of evil. My Father and I will always be the source of life...and the God of surprises.

That's how I'll be for my disciples tonight. I'll see them after supper: they don't expect me to be any place. They won't believe the women when they tell them the good news. They'll stay where they are in Jerusalem, behind locked doors. So I'll have to change my plans. I'd rather they dropped their dismal mood and come running up to Galilee to meet me, but they won't. So I'll surprise them where they are. I'll go back to the city and show them my victory over death, and I'll give them peace.

Once they've been forgiven their sins, they'll become more confident. Then they'll be more alert at last to my ways of grace. They'll be more open to my possibilities.

I want you to be the same. Don't box me in by the pressure points of your moods or your needs for immediate satisfaction. Give me room to strengthen you my way, to alert you for new situations you can't even imagine until you experience them.

This is my Easter message: Be ready for surprises. And the surprise I'll give you will always lead to more life.

I'll no longer tell you of my prayers for you. I already have sent you my Holy Spirit. He'll let you know in prayer how I'm pleading for you to drop those symbols of entombment and decay...and to meet me "someplace else"—in "Galilee."

Love,
Jesus

LETTER 39

Two disciples were going that very day (Easter) to a village named Emmaus...and they were talking about all those things that had happened....Jesus himself drew near and went along with them...but they did not recognize him. And he said to them, "What words were you exchanging as you walk and are sad?" One of them, Cleopas by name, said, "Are you the only stranger in Jerusalem who does not know...concerning Jesus of Nazareth, who was a prophet, mighty in work and word before God and all the people; and how the chief priests and rulers delivered him up to death? We were hoping that it was he who should redeem Israel...but this is the third day since these things came to pass...." But Jesus said to them, "O foolish ones and slow of heart to believe....Did not the Christ have to suffer these things before entering into his glory?"

Luke 24:13-35

*   *   *

Nazareth
Before supper
Friday of Easter Week

Dear Disciple, my Friend,

I've had a lovely day, a quiet day with my mother. This day belonged to just the two of us. Don't know whether you realize it or not, but my new home is heaven now, where I've prepared a place for you (and which I can't adequately describe, as I mentioned before).

Only on occasion do I return to my disciples. There are a few more things that need to be said before my final farewell. I've seen Simon and the other apostles. They're doing fine. I saw hundreds of my disciples yesterday. It'll all be written down. So will the little walk I had with Cleopas and his wife, Mary, at Emmaus.

While my mother's getting supper ready, I want to write you about that experience. Mary of Cleopas is a beautiful person. I'll always be grateful for her courage and compassion, standing by the cross, giving support to my mother. Her husband's a good person, too. Cleopas has been a disciple for almost three years, but he's more easily dejected. He was not as courageous as his wife, but he's a good man just the same.

I want to tell you about this couple. So many people—good people like yourself—are much like them. At a time of crisis, a time of great struggle, when evil is so prevalent you can taste it, good people show their colors as true heroes. There's no time for questioning or brooding. Something needs to be done, something like what Mary of Cleopas did: standing by the cross, being a comforting presence for my mother and a loyal presence to me.

So far, so good. Indeed, very good. But then comes "afterward"; that's when hope breaks down. Bewilderment creeps into the vacuum that's left when all the work is over. When this happens, the soul is open to the most baffling problem since the world began. It will always be the worst of problems and the rock-bottom cause for contention against God: the problem of evil. The words may differ, the situations may differ, but the basic cry is: "How can God—if God is good—permit this evil?"

It was the problem when baby boys were massacred at the time of my birth. It's the question raised with every war, disaster, untimely death, crippling sickness, or hardships caused by exploitation. "Why should it happen?" "If God is good, he'd surely stop such evils! But he does not do so. Therefore, God is not good. He doesn't care, or else he does not exist!"

That's how the anger is expressed. Some people do not go so far as to quit on God, but sometimes they quit on life. That's about as bad.

Such was the case with the couple going to Emmaus. Their afterthoughts about evil bewildered them to the point of quitting. "I was a good man," as they expressed it. "Mighty in works and words among my people." So they couldn't understand how god could permit me to suffer and die—so young—with so much more I could have done. They "hoped" I would be the Messiah. (Their kind of Messiah.) Then their hopes died when I died; so, in a sense, they died too. They gave up on the God-movement I had begun. They were going back home.

I had to instruct them (again!) that the Christ must suffer to enter his glory. I suppose I have to repeat the same instruction for you. With all the letters I've written, I wish this one were superfluous, but it probably isn't. The puzzlement over "a good God permitting evil" is too big a mystery to understand once and for all. God must be honored as good, and evil must be dealt with—both, at the same time. This is difficult.

As you know, I did not solve the problem of evil. I lived through it all during journey to Jerusalem, up to the cross and tomb. I proved my love through suffering, but I did not take away the problem.

Evil will continue. For the most part, suffering is tied up with the human condition. One condition is death—all must die—and sickness is a part of it.

Another human condition is free will. Neither my Father nor I will take away that gift. If humans decide to use their freedom for acts of revenge, war, extortion, or injustice, we won't turn them into stone. We suffer the mayhem done on the people we love. At the end of time, we'll condemn the wicked for their misuse of freedom, but we won't interfere.

After all, God didn't interfere when people vilified my name and scourged my body. Evil was allowed to have its day, yet good came out of it. Because of my passion, no one has anything to fear. You don't have to worry about death, since I've earned life-after-death for you. You don't have to be crushed by persecution, or malice, or any of the hurts that happened to me . . . and will happen to you. I've made a new backdrop for all people. Because of my resurrection, the whole world can see life in a new dimension.

And because of the passion, there is no reason to doubt the mercy of God, my Father . . . no reason to doubt our love. You know these things. Think a minute. It's not from any of my words or cures that you know for certain that I love you; it's because I suffered and died for you that you know this.

So please, my disciple, my friend, don't let desperate situations get you down. I can't appear to every disciple and repeat these reasons for suffering in the world.

Don't walk away from me because you cannot understand why the passion overtakes you. Read my gospel; reread these letters, too. Settle yourself in a place of quiet. Pray about my life and my love; think seriously about such things. Never give up on yourself or my Father, even though evil may seem to have the upper hand.

Do what Cleopas and his wife did: Invite me to stay with you. Let me change the mood of your hopelessness. I'll break bread with you—the bread, which is myself—and give you cause to continue your life of grace and your work of love.

My mother's calling me for supper. Must close now. I beg you to ask her to help you when you're in a crisis. My mother's the best there is. She helped the apostles wait things out; she will help you, also. Farewell.

Love,
Jesus

LETTER 40

While Jesus was eating with them, he charged his disciples not to depart from Jerusalem, but to wait for the promise of the Father: "Wait here in the city and you shall be clothed with power from on high." They then began to ask him, "Lord, will you at this time restore the kingdom to Israel?" But he said to them, "It is not for you to know the times my Father has fixed by his authority; but you shall receive power when the Holy Spirit comes upon you, and you shall be witnesses for me.... And when he had said this, he was lifted up before their eyes, and a cloud took him out of their sight....And they worshipped him, and returned to Jerusalem with great joy. And they were continually...praising and blessing God. Amen.

Luke 1:4-14, 24:36-Conclusion

*   *   *

Jerusalem
Early morning
Ascension Thursday

Dear Disciple, my Friend,

This is my last letter. In a way, I'm relieved. I'm glad I wrote them; it was good for me. It helped focus my trust in God my Father. As I already suggested, writing out thoughts is an excellent form of prayer. I recommend that you write me every now and then. Written words can support your faith; they'll anchor you musings. They'll give me a chance to instruct you.

I'm certain some of my letters helped you, too. They let you understand how your sufferings are much like mine. I hope you reread them as situations come up.

But now my journey is completely over I will send you my Spirit. The Comforter will help and teach you much better than these letters have. Thanks to Pentecost, you will be much more than you could be by yourself. I will be with you...and in you.

I'm waiting for my disciples. They'll soon be here for my last blessing, my last words.

They'll have their last words, too. I'm certain of that! One more time, I'll have to try to get them to let go of their hopes for "painless prospects." They'll ask me if I'm finally going to restore the kingdom. They mean by that to restore things as they used to be, only better—Solomon's splendor...plus! They're really talking about instant paradise, a world where everything is beautiful, peaceful, easy, and trouble-free.

Such a life can't exist, not until they die and come to the new life I've earned for them...and earned for you...and which I presently enjoy.

Meanwhile, back in the proving grounds of love (your world), you'll have to work things out as best you can, even though you're hurting from some of the sorrows mentioned in these letters.

By all means, do everything you can to alleviate pain and injustice. Pray to my Father for healing, and praise the skills of humans for their part in the healing process. Use your time and effort to correct wrongs wherever they occur: in wars, social aggressions, poverty, and unemployment. After all, you'll be judged by that criterion. I identify myself with the poor, the handicapped, the strangers, all those unable to help themselves. The affliction caused by exploitation or by unfair constraint is my affliction, too. When you care for them, you care for me.

Even so, even after all this is understood no one can eliminate the psychological passion. As long as free will lasts, there will be people determined to use their freedom for selfish gain or for vengeful malice. That fondly-wished-for paradise will never exist as long as people continue to hold a grudge, establish cliques, or act competitively with one another.

You must keep living in a less-than-completely-pleasant environment. That's what I'm about to tell my first disciples. That's what I want to tell you, as well.

I am telling you to wait—wait and trust.

The whole story of my life began with that word. My mother was told to wait: "Wait until she was clothed with power from on high." She did. Thanks to her trustful waiting, I was born a human being so that I could feel like you and die for you.

I want you to be like my mother in this. To grow in the spiritual life means mostly that you must wait. In God's time, you'll receive power when my Spirit comes to you. With this power, you'll be able to love spontaneously, to understand the mystery of suffering, to thoroughly enjoy ordinary things like friendship, good meals together, and all the human signs of care and beauty that make your days delightful.

This power by which I could continue on my journey is my gift to you. You'll do new things in new ways, with a new-found enthusiasm.

You'll change your life, as my apostles have changed theirs. From moody, fearful, pessimistic men, they'll return to their city full of joy. And even though they end up martyrs for my sake, they will find they have no room in their hearts for anyting but gratitude to God and the assurance of life after death.

You can do the same. You will. I'll see to it. I have confidence in you. You are the reason for all I've done and suffered during my journey to Jerusalem.

As long as you learn how to "wait for power from on high," you'll know that I'm with you on your journey—that journey that my Father, from all eternity, has prepared for you.

Fare . . . well.

Love,
Jesus

APPENDIX

JESUS VERSUS MAGIC WANDS

There is a battle going on between our Lord's insistence on forceless love and our almost unquenchable desire for a magic wand, something that will somehow make people submit to our wishes.

In a sense, human history presents us with a pageant of magic wands. Clan, tribe, or nation—they never rise to love; they rise to power. Somehow, they discovered an advantage in the martial arts, and they moved with it.

Hannibal had his elephants; Ghengis Khan, his horses; King Arthur, his excalibar sword. Great Britain carved out her Empire thanks to a superior navy and the "British Square." Americans crushed its enemies because they had the bowie knife...then the Springfield rifle...then the machine gun.

Techniques vary, but the story is the same. Thanks to a newly discovered way to intimidate, an oppressor subdues other groups who have not caught on...yet. With superiority on the battlefield, they become chiefs, kings, emperors, colonizers, subjugators.

The world has always been tempted by the same temptation Jesus wrestled with in the desert. (See Letter 35.) The use of power is the quickest, most efficient way to have one's immediate needs satisfied.

On a personal as well as tribal level, we are tempted to use short-cuts or techniques of power in order to make our influence felt.

[Interrupting our Lord's discourse at the Last Supper] "A dispute arose among the disciples as to which of them was to be regarded as the greatest. Jesus said to them: "The kings of the Gentiles exercise lordship over their subjects, and those in authority like to have their influence felt. It shall not be so with you..." (Luke 22: 24-26, see also Mark 10: 42-45; Matthew 20: 25-28).

Many folk tales, comic books, and television programs feed this archetypal longing for a special advantage of some kind: the strength of a spider, the charms of a witch, the knowledge of karate, the Lone

105

Ranger's silver bullets, the invulnerable automobile by which Knight Rider stalks his foes.

Snow White thought that if only she took a bite of the magic apple, she could force Prince Charming to come to her and fulfil her desire for living happily ever after. In *The Wizard of Oz* Dorothy longed for a marvelous country—over the rainbow—where, by simply wishing it to happen, "troubles" would "melt like lemon drops."

Many people who seek help from a friend, counsellor, or priest are not looking for help at all. They want to procure an amulet, a spell to cast on people...some "whammy" by which they can return to their family, fellow workers, or whoever is giving them trouble, and with this new device, they can go "zap!" and instantly cause all their problems to go away.

"If only I could make unpleasant people be more pleasant!" That is the fond wish. "If only I could do to others what Hannibal did to Rome, Ghengis Khan did to Europe, Hitler, with his *blitzkrieg*, did to France, and certain people do to their family when they whine so much, or nag so long, and always get their way. If only there were a magic wand, then troubles would be over, worries would vanish, situations would improve, and I would be much calmer and find life less oppressive!"

It is the universal quest for power. And power is the way most people run their world (and are run by their world). But power is un-Christian. Indeed, it is anti-Christ.

This book was written to demonstrate the truth that love and manipulation cannot co-exist. Forceless love is the only way Jesus lived. That is why he was misunderstood, mocked, and crucified.

It is important to note, however, that he could have used the very kind of power emporers have at their disposal. He could have, but he didn't.

He also could have used all those tricks ordinary people use to "lord it over others." He could have nagged, scolded, moped, used swords or Springfield rifles, or even nuclear bombs, for that matter.

It is important to remember our Lord's final statement about the use of force. It is not included in this book, because we restricted ourselves to St. Luke's Gospel. This passage is in the Gospel of St. Matthew (26: 47-53).

Good Friday morning is the time. The scene is a garden where a squad of soldiers arrested Jesus. Immediately, Simon Peter came to the rescue. He drew his sword. If he had a rifle, or tear gas, he probably would have used that. He happened to have a sword. (It was a symbol of power at that time.)

With a "power stroke," Peter cut off the ear of Malchus, one of the soldiers. This act should have started something. It should have served as a "call to arms." I suppose that's what Peter intended, to begin a general uprising and give Jesus opportunity to escape.

But then a strange thing happened, strange enough to completely deflate Peter and the apostles. They were so crushed by it that they fled.

Jesus refused their forcefulness. He picked up the ear of Malchus, put it back in place, and healed the man instantly.

Then he gave his disciples for all time the severest of reprimands: "Those who live by the sword (the use of power) shall perish by the sword."

Following this, our Lord made one of the most telling pronouncements he ever made: "Don't you know that I could ask my Father and he would, even now, send me twelve armies of angels (. . .to force these soldiers on their knees and frighten them so much that they would have no choice but to honor me?)."

Jesus did have the power to compel, but he refused to use it. He simply loved. And the consequence of forceless love was scorn, imprisonment, false accusation, crucifixion, and death.

He determined to love without conditions; he refused to use force of any kind. Such decisions are bound to lead to suffering.

I wrote this book to spell out the Lord's reprimand to Simon Peter. All through Christ's journey to Jerusalem, he loved in many different ways. He hoped people would respond to his love and was hurt when they refused.

He was helpless in the face of human determination not to be impressed by him. Therefore, he knows from personal experience how we hurt from the same forms of suffering.

I thought it well to add this appendix as a postscript to remind me and my readers that our Lord could have used force, if he wanted to.

Otherwise, it might be thought that he was simply helpless because the people who hated him were too powerful for him. Not so. He was helpless before hatred because he chose to be, because he chose to love.

If we are true followers of Christ, we will love as he did. We will continue, despite our psychological passion. And we will refuse to make use of any "magic wand," even the most secret weapons in our arsenal of manipulative tricks.